Ten Reasons:
Finding Balance on Environmental Issues

Paul H. Betancourt

Table of Contents

Foreword

P aul Betancourt writes a thoughtful and compelling book on the conflicts facing farmers and environmentalists. I've known Paul for many years as a hard working family farmer who did not come by this profession, in the traditional way. His birthplace and where he was raised, New York City, is a long ways from the farming fields in the San Joaquin Valley agriculture communities in California.

Sadly today, the effort to successfully farm and produce cost effective, healthy foods for America's dinner table, is taken for granted by the majority of Americans.

One of my biggest gripes is that many in the environmental community do not understand a basic simple fact that farmers are price takers not price makers. From the Capitol in Sacramento to the Oval Office I have shared this message. Paul tries to explain that every new regulation or law that is enacted, where a cost is involved, there is no ability to pass that cost to the beneficiary not withstanding best of intentions. Farmers have to absorb those costs.

It's my view that America's farmers are among the best environmentalists in the country. Why, you might ask? Because the sustainability of their land is directly related to their ability to farm. The quality and the safety of the food they produce is directly related to the price they get in the marketplace. And don't forget farmers, their families, and their workers are consumers too.

Paul will tell you, "you can't fake farming!" His book gives a candid assessment on the challenges America's farm family's face. While some folks in the cities may hang onto a romantic notion about rural life in America, the bottom line is that it's a lot of hard work and risk taking.

This is recommended reading for those who want to better understand why American agriculture is so exasperated by many in the environmental community.

Jim Costa
United States House of Representatives
D-Fresno

Ten Reasons-
Introduction

What does this farmer thinks of the environment?

I love it! One reason I chose to farm was to be able to work *in* and *with* the natural world. Farmers don't seem to get enough of the outdoors. When we do get time off, it is not unusual to find us hunting, fishing, water skiing or snow skiing. Horseback riding and rodeo are other ways we spend our off-time outdoors. Now-a-days motorcycles have been added to the list. My favorite days are spent outdoors. Some of my favorite trips were to the Sierra high country or at the coast. A quiet evening on the back porch with a book and a cup of coffee is a great way to end my day.

Unlike most farmers, I wasn't born into a farm family. I am the first in my family to farm in five generations. I chose to leave town and move to the country. I like what Thoreau wrote about going to Walden,

> *"I went to the woods because I wished to live deliberately, to front only the essential facts of life, and see if I could not learn what it had to teach, and not, when I came to die, discover that I had not lived"* (Thoreau 8).

Part of the reason I went to the farm was to see if I could learn what nature had to teach me.

Working landscapes-

One thing that separates me from your garden variety environmentalist is that I make my living from my interaction with the natural world. Our farm is a working landscape. I have to balance care for the environment with producing something. Most environmentalists have no responsibility to produce anything so it is easy for them to be one dimensional about the environment. This distinction is at the very heart of the tension between farmers and environmentalists. I have a pragmatic and utilitarian view of my farm. Environmentalists tend to romanticize nature in general and farms in particular. I like to romanticize nature too. I have hiked and camped up in the Sierra High country and visited national parks overseas. Additionally, my faith teaches me that we have the role of caretakers of the environment. We are unlike any other species. For example, I do not see coyotes requesting hunting permits for rabbits. Whether it is by mere awareness or by divine mandate, as a species we have a responsibility unlike any other species to care for the environment.

It cannot be a case of production first or protection first. This is why I advocate balance. If production is given sole first priority then some will take that as permission to rape and pillage the environment and shrug at the consequences. If protection is given sole first priority then we will never get anything accomplished. The Precautionary Principle will be invoked and tie us in knots. We need a healthy environment <u>and</u> a healthy economy. They are not necessarily mutually exclusive.

While I have a pragmatic view of the nature on my farm as a working landscape, I do so with a deep sense of wonder. I get to experience the miracle of seeds every season. There is a lot of work that goes into preparing a field for planting. We begin months ahead of time- tilling the soil, furrowing out the beds, irrigating the field then cultivating weeds. Then the big day comes and we open the first sack of seed. Remember, there is a lot riding on this- a whole season's crop starts at planting and there is rarely any way to make up for lost time.

Inside those seeds is the miracle of life. We could do all the same work and if we plant pebbles or jelly beans nothing would happen. But, we plant seeds- and if the conditions are right they sprout. I get to witness this miracle every Spring. There is nothing like seeing the first plants sprout out of the ground on a warm Spring day. I know I am off to a good start. Patrick Holden, a farmer in the UK, says "Agriculture is a dance with nature" (Garcia). That is a great image.

To farm well you have to know your partner, and know the rhythm. It is a wonder to behold when the dance goes well.

In a very real sense, I do not grow anything. In our area farmers are often called 'growers', but we don't really "grow" anything. At best, I make the most of the conditions of sunshine, rainfall me it is a miracle.

Farming is a partnership with the natural world. If farmers can understand enough of how the natural world works and try to cooperate with nature they can make a living. I cannot plant cotton in January, it is too cold. I cannot plant my cotton in July, that is too late to produce a crop before winter. I cannot force nature. If I plant at the proper time, I have the potential to make a crop.

Most people in our society are insulated from the natural world. Whether you work in an office, a classroom, a manufacturing plant or a retail store, you have artificial lights and climate control. [Think about that phrase for a moment. We used to have heating and air conditioning. Now we call it climate control.] Your work schedule doesn't change drastically if it is raining or the sun is shining. Of course, snow or heavy rain might affect getting to and from work, but that is another story. In fact, it highlights how insulated most of us are from the natural world.

Being insulated from the natural world makes it easy to idealize or romanticize nature. Growing up in San Diego, to me the natural world was a day at the beach or a hike with the Boy Scouts. Nature was a fabulous break from life in the city and suburbs. I was fascinated. In high school I started preparing to major in biology or marine biology in college.

I took another path after meeting a nice girl whose family farmed. We only planned to stay on the farm for a few years. Thirty years later we are still here. One of the things I have realized is what I have tried to share here. I have a different view of nature because I farm. I cannot romanticize nature like I used to, like many people do today. Neither can I be totally pragmatic about nature. I am in awe and wonder about the miracles of nature and the partnership we have with nature to grow our food.

Killing the Goose That Laid the Golden Egg

As a kid, I remember reading the old Aesop Fable about the king who had a goose that laid a golden egg every morning. The king got greedy and wanted all the eggs at once. So, he killed the goose and cut it open thereby losing the goose that laid the golden eggs. The moral, usually, is that it is bad to be greedy, which is a good lesson. There is another way to interpret the fable. How good were the king's problem solving skills? He really didn't understand what was happening, did he?

I fear as a society we are killing the goose that lays the golden eggs. In this case the golden eggs are the benefits of modern life. I understand the criticism of modern life. I could add some of my own criticisms. But, the fact is, I like modern life. I like sleeping indoors at night and having running water. The people of the world like modern life too. People in developing countries don't aspire to be tree hugging vegans. They aspire to what modern life has to offer. There is a reason we like modern life- we like longer and healthier life spans and a higher material standard of living. We like getting away from the drudgery of hunter-gatherers or subsistence farming. Lomborg notes that our life spans have extended from 30 years at the turn of the last century to well over 67 years now (Lomborg 4). Every parent appreciates that the infant mortality rate has also dropped over fifty percent in the last century (Lomborg 53). We like modern life, which is good because as Wallace Kaufmann reminds us, "there is no turning back" (Kaufmann 14).

There have been massive and horrid environmental problems since the beginning of the Industrial Age. The problems accelerated after World War Two. In the late 60's and early 70's Americans recoiled at the trash on the roads, smokestacks belching in our air and rivers catching on fire. We knew that couldn't be good. We recoiled from these disasters and we are committed to changing how we produce our products and how we live our lives. We passed-

The Clean Air Act (1972)
The Clean Water Act (1977)
The Endangered Species Act (1969)
and we created the Environmental Protection Agency (1970)

Caring for our neglected environment became a guiding principle and the pendulum swung away from the excesses that caused those problems.

I think the pendulum has swung too far and we are in danger of killing the goose that lays the golden eggs of modern life. We are in danger of being the first generation to lower life spans and lower our standard of living. Please, don't get me wrong. I accept the government's role in regulating business. Arthur Schlesinger Jr. notes that since the time of Andrew Jackson, "the public conscience, in the form of the democratic government, had to step in to prevent the business community from tearing society apart in the pursuit of profit" (Schlesinger 510).

I get it. I am not asking for government to keep their hands off. Of course there are days I think that would be a good idea, but that is another dialogue. What I am asking for are reasonable rules and regulations. Let's do some real problem solving instead of filing lawsuits and piling on regulations.

Manufacturers are criticized for moving jobs offshore. They are accused of going after cheaper labor. Have you considered they might be trying to avoid the burden of over regulation? I sure have. As a farmer there are days when I wish I could move my farm. You should see some of the ideas that come our way. One suggestion from the government agencies that we created to "help" was that we water every dirt road in our county, every day to keep the dust down- even if no one drove on that road. Do you have any idea how many miles of dirt roads there are in our county?

I live in fear of a $10,000 fine for not filling out some form correctly. Lest you think I am overreacting, I once had a bureaucrat tell me to shut my farm down because I had not put up a newly required labor poster. The irony was I had called him to get the new poster. He told me he couldn't give me a poster to make me compliant, but I should shut the farm down until I had the poster. My wife and I have started calling these 'Death of Common Sense Experiences' after reading Phillip Howard's book "The Death of Common Sense." Howard records dozens of these kinds of experiences. Many farmers have experienced their own "death of common sense" experiences on environmental issues. These kinds of events make us cynical about the environmental movement and the whole regulatory system.

I would like to restore common sense to our public dialogue on environmental issues.

-Environmentalists who take water for their city from a dam in a national park get an automatic discount in credibility.
-Nuclear power cannot be bad in the US and good in France. Either nuclear power is good and part of our energy future, or we stop congratulating the French for being good environmentalists.
-It does not make sense to want organic food because you are scared of pesticides and then chain smoke like some of my Italian friends.

We need some common sense in our public dialogue on environmental issues. There has been enough silliness from all sides. We need safe and sane environmental policy. Ultimately I am confident we can balance a healthy environment and a healthy economy, but not if we continue to get stuck in ironic 'Death of Common Sense" experiences.

The environmentalists won the basic argument a generation ago. As a society we are committed to caring for the planet. No one is asking permission to pollute. The question is, how do we get past the log jam we have now?

Most environmental policy discussions that I have been involved in are confrontational. When I was sixteen, I joined the Sierra Club. At my first meeting everyone was saying, "Well, we beat the nuclear guys on that issue. Who do we go after next?" That was also my last Sierra Club meeting. As a starry eyed idealist, I was surprised there was no problem solving dialogue.

Things have not changed over the decades. I have gone to public hearings where no one was listening. Politicians were grandstanding for the news. Journalists were searching for sound bites. Activists were shouting to be heard. But, very little listening, very little dialogue was done. Each side just tossed verbal hand grenades at each other.

I have sat as a gubernatorial appointee, receiving testimony that had nothing to do with the issue at hand, just so folks could get something off their chests. That may have been therapeutic for them, but it didn't get us any closer to solving the problem. (The problem at hand was nitrates from dairies getting into the groundwater. That is a serious concern. But, their own data showed the nitrate plumes were miles from the dairies in question. Then, they brought up the fact that there was arsenic in the drinking water of some rural communities. I would be concerned about that also. But, no one has ever suggested any arsenic has ever come from the dairies in question.) I appreciate the concern my rural neighbors have about their water quality. We bought bottled water for a house we rented because the well had DBCP in it. But, that kind of testimony is like a red herring in a detective novel, it is a distraction. We don't need any more distractions. We need good information to make good environmental policy.

An Assumption

I realize there are implied assumptions in what I am saying. One assumption is modern life is good. This is a philosophical assumption worthy of much discussion. But, we do not have time for a full-scale debate on that issue here.

I, for one, like the benefits of modern medicine and reduction in drudgery that we have in the modern world. I can flick my laundry in the washing machine and do something else instead of wandering down to the creek and beat my clothes on a rock all day. I'll give up my cell phone and the Internet long before I would give up my washing machine. I appreciate that our life spans have nearly doubled in the last century and as a parent I like that the infant mortality rate has been cut in half. I didn't have to watch one of my children die of a preventable disease like my grandparents did.

At a conference in 1995 in Long Beach, California futurist Jennifer James talked about forces that are changing our world today-

Changes in technology,
  lead to changes in economics.
Changes in economics,
  lead to changes in demographics.
Changes in demographics,
  Lead to changes in culture.

For an example, let's look at my profession, farming. The introduction of tractors and electric motors cut the need for hand labor. The reduction in heavy hand labor led to a migration from our farms to our cities over the last century changing our national demographics. The shift from a farm centered population to an urban centered population has changed our culture.

We can argue endlessly whether this change was a good thing or not. The point is, as James points out, that a given change in technology will work its way down through our society and change our culture.

There are countless other examples from medicine to computers to telecommunications that have made fundamental change to our culture. There is no stopping the wave of the future. As Kaufmann writes, we really don't want to stop that wave. We like the benefits of modern life. Instead of trying to turn the clock back, the smart approach is to deal with the problems and move on.

But, I am a qualified supporter of progress. I don't swallow the idea whole. As an Idealist, I am not impressed with materialism and its child, consumerism. Let's be real for a moment; our concern for the environment is how our Western, consumer lifestyles affect the natural world. It is constantly changing fashion, 'disposable this' and 'instant that' which are spoiling our landscape with garbage and overflowing our landfills.

A Word About Irony-

I would like to address the issue of irony. I use the term 'ironic' quite often. I find it ironic that US environmentalists hate nuclear power and love France, which gets most of its electricity from nuclear power plants. I could say the enviros are hypocritical, but I will give them the benefit of the doubt. I think that often in their passion for their cause they lose a little perspective. This would hardly be worth comment except for the fact that the environmental movement has so much impact on public policy. I have noticed that not only do today's enviros have the zeal of religious converts they also have their own sacred places, sacred times, sacred writings and moral code, which they would like all of us to follow. But, that too is a discussion for another time.

Soren Kierkegaard was a master of irony. In fact, his dissertation was titled, "The Concept of Irony." As a philosopher SK was the founder of modern existentialism. Because of his status as a philosopher and his broadside against the church many people assume he was a skeptic. Actually, SK was a man of profound faith. He holds up the

Knight of Faith as an ideal (Kierkegaard 38ff). His comments on the parables of Jesus are full of wit and warmth. His <u>Christian Discourses</u> is a neglected classic. His writing can be so difficult to read that many Christians don't bother and most skeptics ignore his position on faith.

Kierkegaard used irony to highlight the inconsistencies of the dominant social power of his day- the Danish state church. In one story he writes how a preacher in Copenhagen read the Gospel story of Jesus telling His followers to give up everything and follow Him. Then the preacher, clad in an elegant robe, closed the gilt Bible with a velvet bookmark, in a stain glass church- and no one laughed. Kierkegaard didn't criticize the church as an outsider, he was a man of deep faith. He pointed out the sad ironies of a church that didn't live up to its own ideals.

A dominant social power in our world today is the environmental movement. Cross it and the wrath of its followers will come down on you. For example, if you have doubts about global climate change you can be branded a 'global warming denier'. Use of this terminology tries to put doubters of climate change, which is at best a scientific theory, on the same level of those who doubt the Holocaust, which is established historic fact. Only a fool or someone with a serious political agenda would deny the Holocaust. But, I for one have my questions about climate change that are based in science and reason. The reasonable thing to do would be to address my questions rationally, not resort to name calling or labeling.

I am merely using SK's tool of irony to highlight the inconsistencies of the environmental movement. Like SK, I do this as a loving believer. I like clean air and clean water. I believe there is more to life than making a buck. I believe we have a divine mandate to care for the natural world. I believe we can balance a healthy environment and a healthy economy. In fact, I believe it is imperative that we do so. However, like religious legalists of previous generations today's environmentalists are in danger of losing their credibility because of their ironic inconsistencies.

Finding Balance

If we are going to care for the environment, let's do it right. In the concluding chapter I will lay out some principles that can bring us back on track. The primary principle is balancing the economy and the environment.

We have not lost our sense of purpose. We have lost our sense of balance. One way to learn balance is to have some perspective. The problem with the current fad of living in the moment is that we have lost perspective on so many things. We see everything in isolation. You can have a car, a telephone, a home, a refrigerator, air

conditioning and still be considered poor in America. Do you know what the poverty line is in India? When I went there in '96 they said the poverty line in India was 2500 calories. If you had 2500 calories of food a day- no house, no car, no phone, no TV- just 2500 calories of food per day, you were above the poverty line. That puts things in perspective doesn't it?

It doesn't help that the 24 hour news cycle drives this even further. "If it bleeds it leads." My Dad pointed out how one San Diego news station opened their evening news with a fire every night. If there wasn't one in San Diego they found one somewhere else . One night we watched the local news together and they opened with a fire- in Iowa. They couldn't find a fire in San Diego, or, apparently, in all of California. We have lost perspective.

I teach world religions at the college level. One of the things I have learned to appreciate from the Asian religions and philosophies is their idea of balance. It would do us great good if we could gain a measure of balance when it comes to the environment. If we ever needed balance, now is the time. We will not voluntarily turn our back on modern life. On the other hand we must find reasonable ways to care for the natural world.

The Ten Reasons in this book came from an op-ed I published a few years ago. You can find the original essay in the Appendix. The headers for each chapter come from the original essay.

Reason Ten:

Natural Resources

#10-I'll start believing San Francisco environmentalists when they stop taking their drinking water from a national park.

This chapter is about more than water. What is at issue is the use of natural resources. In the American West one of the largest natural resource issues is water; water for farms and water for cities. There are other natural resource issues we must address on a national and global scale such as; coal, natural gas, timber and even rock quarried for road construction.

One of the biggest ironies in environmental policy, that I have personally experienced, is that San Francisco takes over *eighty one billion gallons per year* of water out of a national park, transports it hundreds of miles across our valley, uses it once and flushes it out to the ocean. Then I have had San Francisco environmental attorneys lecture me on water conservation and how if we were more careful with our water supply we wouldn't have the water quality issues we have in our valley. Unbelievable. I could solve some real water quality issues here in the San Joaquin Valley if I could have that quarter million acre feet that San Francisco uses to utilize our area.

In California, two thirds of the rainfall is north of Sacramento and two thirds of the people live in the southern part of state. As Marc Reisner noted in <u>Cadillac Desert</u>, that is the kind of fact that caused us to build an artificial, four hundred mile long river that runs uphill (Reisner 345).

The enviros can say what they want, but among farmers and farm-workers in my area the question of how to utilize natural resources has come down to the question- people or fish? In 2009, when water supplies were cut to protect endangered species, an economic study by UC Davis found sixty to eighty thousand people lost their jobs due to the water supply cuts (Howitt et. al 2). You can understand why my neighbors see this as a 'people vs. fish' scenario.

The deeper question, of course, is *what is the proper use of natural resources*? I asked this question of one of my grad school professors, who is a self-proclaimed radical environmentalist. His response was, "no one has the answer to this question."

In one sense, that answer is probably correct. No one can precisely quantify how much of a natural resource we can utilize before it is 'too much.' Additionally, some resources are by nature not renewable. When we mine gold, or diamonds we really don't grow another crop of those, do we?

In another sense previous generations had no problem answering this question, at least in principle. Gifford Pinchot headed the US Forestry Bureau and the US Natural Conservation Commission for Theodore Roosevelt a century ago (Roosevelt 409, 424). Roosevelt said of Pinchot, "He led and indeed during its most vital period embod-ied the fight for *the preservation through use of our forests*" (Roosevelt 409, italics mine). Pinchot's principle was, that we may and must utilize natural resources as long as we do not destroy them and their ability to renew themselves. Today's environmentalists preach, "Reduce, reuse and renew" as a guiding principle. Few realize that previous genera-tions practiced this principle on a large scale. As Solomon said, "There is nothing new under the sun" (Ecclesiastes 1:9-11).

Timber harvest is still a good example of renewable resource utilization. Except for extreme enviros, we agree that you can harvest timber as long as you replant trees, thereby renewing the resource over time. An example is what we see in places like Southern Sweden. On my first trip there I noticed beautiful forests along the road sides. After a while, I realized that the trees were uniform in size and age. That's not natural. Subsequently, I found out through my Swedish cousins and some fellow Rotarians, that wood and paper products are some of the largest exports from Sweden. The Swedes deeply love the natural world *and* the Swedes have developed a system of long term natural resource utilization. Some of these forests are left in place thirty to seventy years before they are logged. Sometimes the person who plants the trees never gets to see them harvested. The Swedes have developed a methodical, long term system utilizing timber as a natural resource. The Swedes, who are very environmentally conscious, generally all support this use of their natural resources.

The contrast with Gifford Pinchot comes from his same era in the person of John Muir. Where Pinchot sought to create sustainable use of a renewable resource, Muir and his followers believe we have no right to use any natural resources if there is any negative impact on other species. Of course the irony here is that Muir's first jobs in his beloved Sierras included herding sheep and managing a timber mill in Yosemite (Muir *x*). To his credit, Muir did help with the creation of the national park system and his last battle was fighting the creation of the reservoir in Yosemite National Park that feeds water to San Francisco today. This is just a reminder of how difficult finding balance can be. A world famous conservationist spent part of his life herding sheep and sawing lumber. As Schweitzer says, "I am life which wills to live in the midst of life which wills to live" (Joy 248).

Pinchot's principles of resource use dominated the first half of the Twentieth Century. Since the 60's and 70's Muir's spiritual heirs have dominated the debate on natural resource issues. Their answer is a resounding "No!" if there is any risk to any natural resource. This is a noble sentiment, but it is unnatural and impractical. It is unnatural in that no other life lives by this principle. Coyotes don't file hunting permits when they chase rabbits. Beavers don't file Environmental Impact Reports when they build dams. You can argue we are more intelligent than coyotes and beavers. There are days I that might argue with you on that point, but I do agree we are more aware of our impacts and that awareness brings responsibility. That being said, I side with Pinchot over Muir on the use of natural resources. I side with Pinchot, not because I am a farmer and I want to irrigate my crops, but because I also use other resources and this is the sane alternative. Of course Muir is right and there are places like Yosemite and Yellowstone that should be protected for future generations to enjoy. But, Pinchot has the balanced perspective. No one is asking permission to rape and pillage the environment.

Pinchot gave us principles and the example of forestry: "use and renew". Those principles are even more important today.

In Muir and Pinchot's day there were two million Californians and ninety two million Americans. Today there are over thirty five million Californians and three hundred million Americans. There are more of us with an even higher standard of living than a century ago.

The natural resource issue in the West, is water. It is hard to explain to those of you in the Mid West or Eastern part of the US how important water is in the West. [Perhaps a map might help. Notice how east of the Rockies it is basically green? Looking at the left it is basically brown. This reflects the difference in rainfall and the dry climate in the West.] When writing about the establishment of the Bureau of Reclamation in 1902, President Theodore Roosevelt said his purpose was "reclaiming the waste areas of the arid West by irrigating lands otherwise worthless, and creating new homes upon the land" (Roosevelt 411). We can quibble over the value of "new homes on the land". Roosevelt obviously came from a different era. But, the results speak for themselves. Water projects did change the face of the West and not just for farmers. I suspect that California would still only have about two million people if it weren't for the water projects. Even in TR's life the results were obvious. Roosevelt wrote, "This Act and the results flowing from it have helped powerfully prove to the Nation that it can handle its own resources and exercise direct and business-like control over them" (Roosevelt 413).

I can already see some of my environmental friends rolling their eyes over that last statement. Recently (March 2010) I was in Palo Alto for an annual meeting of an environmental group with which I am involved. One casual comment went unchallenged, "the problem is a small part of our water is used for people's needs and the majority is used to make money." Wow! Because that statement reflects the perception of many people it is worth looking at in detail.

The basic stats are that California averages about 80-100 million acre feet (MAF) per year. Of that 100MAF of rainfall about 31MAF is used for human activity; 24 MAF for irrigation and 7 MAF for homes and businesses (California Water Institute 4). Remember what Disraeli said, "There are three types of lies; lies, damned lies and statistics." Let's look at these numbers carefully. What this woman said in our meeting in Palo Alto is a common perception. Farmers do use the vast majority of the *developed* water. (Developed water is the water stored and utilized for farms and cities. It is a fraction of the total rainfall.) There is no debate about that. There are two important points that get lost in that perception.

First, far more water goes into the environment than ever goes to Ag. Only 27% of the state's water is used by irrigation. The majority, as is proper, nourishes our forests and fills our streams and rivers.

Second, who is the end user of the water used for irrigation? Is the farmer the end user? Or, is the consumer the end user? I think the consumer is the end user. If the consumer is the end user that means someone back East eating one of the cantaloupes or almonds grown on my farm has a profound interest in water issues in California.

Natural resource issues are important to all of us, even if you have never been on a farm. Because we all have a stake in natural resource issues, it is important we pay attention and get them right. This is important public policy and we have this amazing system of self-government where we have a say in what happens

If you think government policy is not important consider this-the 1998 Nobel Prize winner in Economics was won by an Indian economist, Amartya Sen, for proving governments cause famines. If governments can cause famines and kill its own people in the slowest way possible- by starvation, we can see how important public policy can be. Sen notes not all famines are caused by droughts, but even when famines are caused by droughts, "droughts may not be avoidable but their affects can be" (Sen 123).

Writing a century and a half before Sen, another economist wrote,

"Whoever examines, with attention, the history of dearths and famines which have affected any part of Europe, during the course of the present or preceding two centuries...will find...that a famine never arises from any other cause but the violence of government attempting, by improper means, to remedy the inconveniences of dearth" (Smith 363).

I digress a bit, but my point is to highlight the importance of what is at stake. Water policy is not just a fight between the farmers and the environmentalists, water policy is not just a Californian or Western issue. Water policy is not, in a real sense merely an American issue. If we can get water policy in California right, we not only solve the problem on my farm, we have also created a model of natural resource use for the whole world.

Reason Nine:

Energy

#9- I'll start believing the French on energy and environmental issues when they turn off their nuclear reactors. Either nuclear power is bad, or it is good. Nuclear power cannot be good in France and bad in the US.

Ten years ago California went through a mini power crisis. Through a combination of foolish legislation and greedy power companies, California experienced rolling blackouts and spikes in energy prices. During this time, one of the things I realized is that **we have more people using more energy all the time**. Think about it. When I was a kid, back in the Stone Age, homes had one TV and one telephone, with no answering machine- they didn't even exist. Fax machines and personal computers were not even dreamed of yet. My high school classmates had to play their computer games, one move per day, on the school district's mainframe computer, and that was innovative and cutting edge.

Today, how often do you see a teen without an iPod stuffed in their ears or tapping out a text message? Our homes are filled with TVs, computers, wireless phones, cell phones, and MP3 players. Not only do most homes have more than one TV now, the TVs have satellite dishes and DVRs attached to them. Offices are stuffed with computers, fax machines, paper shredders and other tools. We have GPS units for our cars that need chargers. *These all take electrons, lots of electrons.* In my day, cash registers were mechanical and credit cards were crunched on that hand machine that made a carbon copy of the receipt. Now cash registers are flat screens and credit cards are read with a swipe of the hand. All that takes more electrons. According to the US Department of Energy, U.S. demand for electricity will grow by another fifty percent by 2025 (Cravens 362). *Global demand for electricity is expected to grow by 160% in the next forty years!* (Cravens 365).

All of this is going on and we cannot seem to be able to agree on how to make more energy. We agree strip mining and burning coal is not the best idea. But, we try alternatives and that is where we run into trouble. We have hydro power, but there is opposition to damming rivers. Billions of dollars were spent on wind farms in California during the Carter and Reagan years and then the windmills were left to sit idle for years. Someone found birds were getting caught in the windmill blades. The enviros never liked nuclear power- then Three Mile Island happened. Instead of learning lessons from Three Mile Island they just shut that option down for decades, while we had more people using more energy all the time.

Every alternative that was provided was shut down, even solar. We like solar, we just cannot decide where to put it. The desert seems like a good place to gather solar energy. There is plenty of sunlight in the desert. But, putting solar energy farms in the desert is protested because there are endangered species and wildlife habitat there. Instead of offering solutions or even principles for reasonable solutions, the enviros simply say, "No" to nearly every alternative that is offered. The result? After forty years of discussion on the subject the US is still burning huge amounts of coal. Forty years after the 1973 Energy Crisis we are importing an even higher percentage of our oil from overseas. What was Einstein's famous definition of insanity? Doing the same thing and expecting different results.

I am not a big fan of the logic that says we should do everything just because the Europeans do it, but in this case I will make an exception. It is generally accepted that the French get 60%, or more, of their electricity from nuclear power. Other European countries follow suit. Germany and Finland, for example, are big consumers of nuclear power. Nuclear power cannot be good in France and bad in the US.

I realize the risks of nuclear power. As I have been writing this chapter in March of 2011 Japan has suffered a huge earthquake and is wrestling with a near catastrophic problem with their Fukushima nuclear power plant. Before I go on about the possibilities of nuclear power let's take a moment and consider the lessons to be learned from Fukushima.

First, the power plant at Fukushima survived a 9.0 earthquake and automatically shut down according to its design. It is hard for those of us who have never experienced a 9.0 earthquake to imagine what that is like. With all of that the reactors were shaken, not stirred. The crisis with the Fukushima power plants was not caused by the earthquake but by the tsunami that followed and drowned out the power supply for the plants themselves.

The second thing to remember is that the Fukushima power plants were thirty years old and their design was on the order of fifty years old. Consider how cars, computers and phones have changed in the last thirty years. We learn. Technology changes and improves. Experts in the press have been quoted as saying that modern, gravity fed water cooling systems at Fukushima would have avoided the problems they had there. The idea of gravity fed water cooling systems didn't even exist when those plants were built. We grow, we learn, we adapt. My favorite Clint Eastwood movie is "Heartbreak Ridge". Clint's character, Gunnery Sergeant Tom Highway, teaches a Recon unit to "Adapt, innovate and overcome." That is the kind of can-do attitude that is missing in our environmental debates.

I don't want to brush off concerns about nuclear power. Nuclear power has significant risks. But, I don't think those risks mean we impose the Precautionary Principle and ban the use of the technology. We should learn from our experience. We will learn from Fukushima. We are already learning. Future plants will be even safer than the Fukushima plant which withstood a 9.0 earthquake. (We will talk about the Precautionary Principle more in Reason 4).

It is ultimately ironic that the renewed interest in nuclear power comes from our concern for humanity's carbon foot print. Recovering environmentalists like Stewart Brand and Gwyneth Cravens now support the safe use of nuclear power because they see nuclear power as good for the environment. We live in a time when the major concern of most environmentalists is global climate change. The concern is that the increased CO_2 levels since the beginning of the Industrial Revolution may have a Greenhouse Effect and cause major changes in global weather patterns. Energy production for electricity is one of the major sources of these potential greenhouse gases. One way to cut the production of greenhouse gases is to switch electricity production from coal and natural gas to nuclear. Both Brand and Cravens have written and spoken publicly in support of nuclear power.

Stewart Brand was one of the founders of the Whole Earth Catalogue back in the late 60's and early 70's. He has spent his life on various environmental projects and crusades. In his 2009 book, The Whole Earth Discipline, Brand writes, "With global warming the game has changed" (Brand 105). The threat from greenhouse gases is so large in Brand's mind that we must consider alternatives like the long hated nuclear power. Brand goes step-by-step through the objections that have been raised by the environmental community over the decades and answers each one. Nuclear waste? We can deal with nuclear waste now, and our technology for dealing with it in the future will be even better.

Brand quotes the late Anglican Bishop Hugh Montefiore who served as a trustee of the UK Friends of the Earth before stepping down.

The future of the planet is more important than membership of the Friends of the Earth...The real reason why the Government has not taken up the nuclear option is because it lacks public acceptance, due to the scare stories in the media and the stonewalling opposition of powerful environmental organizations. Most, if not all, of the objections do not stand up to objective assessment (Brand 87).

Of course, Montefiore was pilloried by the environmental community for taking this position.

Brand quotes an article from *Psychology Today* titled "Ten Ways We Get the Odds Wrong".

We fear spectacular, unlikely events...

We underestimate threats that creep up on us...Risk arguments cannot be divorced from values...

We love sunlight, but fear nuclear power...the word radiation stirs thoughts of nuclear power, x-rays, and danger, so we shudder at the thought of erecting nuclear power plants in our neighborhoods. But, every day we're bathed in radiation that has killed more people than nuclear reactors: sunlight.

It's hard to grasp the danger because sunlight feels so familiar and natural.

We should fear fear itself. Though the odds of dying in a terror attack like 9/11 or contracting Ebola are infinitesimal, the effects of chronic stress caused by constant fear are significant (Brand 91-2).

John Stossel makes similar arguments when he asks, "Are we scaring ourselves to death?

Gwyneth Cravens is a novelist and 80's era nuclear protestor. She helped shut down the Shoreham Nuclear Power Plant project on Long Island (Brand 80). The two key issues for Cravens are "footprint and baseload". "Footprint" is the amount of space a particular energy system takes up. "Baseload" is the constant requirement to keep the lights of our society on. Regarding "footprint" Cravens writes, "A nuclear power plant producing 1,000 megawatts takes up a third of a square mile. A wind farm would have to cover over 200 square miles to obtain the same result, and a solar array over 50 square miles" (Cravens 16). Regarding "baseload", alternative energy has consequences of their own. The prime issue is they do not have the capacity to produce a regular supply of energy to meet our baseload needs. Solar and wind are probably part of our energy future, but only as a niche. Solar doesn't work at night and wind doesn't work on calm days. We need a constant supply of energy for the modern world.

We have more people using more energy every day; not just in California, but around the world. Brand quotes a South African activist organization, Abahlali baseMjondolo,

Electricity is not a luxury. It is a basic right. It is essential for children to do their homework; for safe cooking and heating; for people to charge phones, to be able to participate in the national debate through electronic communication…for lighting to keep women safe and, most of all to stop the fires that terrorize us (Brand116).

As a classical political scientist, I might question if electricity is a political right, but I whole heartedly agree electricity is essential to modern life.

Reason Eight:

Where does our food come from?

#8-I'll start believing Europeans about organic farming when they stop chain smoking. [I am constantly amazed how my European friends are so concerned about possible carcinogens in their food and yet they are such heavy smokers.]

One of the more interesting travel conversations I have ever had was when visiting Italy. We were part of a Sister City group visiting Verona. When our hosts found out I was the token farmer of the group, I got peppered with questions about "biological" foods. I kept scratching my head, "biological foods?" I thought all foods were biological by definition. Obviously something was being lost in translation. Finally the light went on- they were asking about organic food. OK, now the question made sense, especially since we were in Italy at the time of the Mad Cow scare in Great Britain. Our trip was timed for the annual Ag show in Verona. There was a huge empty area at the show where all the livestock usually went. Verona hosts one of the largest Ag shows in Europe, but half of the displays were missing because of the concern about Mad Cow disease. People were scared about their food. The irony in this case was the people who were peppering me with questions about organic food were chain smoking cigarettes. There was definitely a disconnect.

For starters, let me say, no one could want to grow organically more than I do.

Remember, I grew up in suburban Southern California with all the idealism about farming I could muster. In addition to that we live on one of our ranches and we raised our kids on the farm. You can bet I don't apply anything around my home that isn't safe. Over the years, I have participated in university trials to study organic pest control methods on our farm. We have run our own test plots. We have spread tons of manure. I have gone to workshops and conferences on organic farming. We have tried all of this to explore ways to incorporate organic methods on my farm. If there is a way to do it I want to know about it. So far, I haven't figured out how to make it work on my farm without going broke.

Now let's address this notion that organic food is better than conventional food, that organic is more virtuous than conventional.

First, a neighbor of mine makes a good living producing raw, organic milk. He is quite a cheerleader for the virtues of raw milk. I have seen him wind up and go at the local farmers market. It is a sight to behold. He would make any pitch man, tent revival preacher or politician proud. Heck, he would make P.T. Barnum proud. He is a passionate, true believer in the virtue of raw milk, and that is great. I have also talked with him in private. In private he will admit the whole organic thing is a marketing tool. Some people are willing to pay more for organic. That's fine with me. My problem with our organic neighbors is that they can't seem to sell their product without bad mouthing my product, and that is a problem.

Of course, no one wants tainted food, I get it. But, that is not what we are talking about here. First, properly grown conventional food is perfectly safe. You might not realize it, but <u>every</u> application of <u>every</u> pest control material on <u>every</u> field in California is reported to the state. This reporting alone takes a lot of effort. Thank Heaven for the Internet because it has made the paperwork so much easier. You can imagine how many forms it would take to record every application on every field in the state. The goal is to have a field-to-fork record of how your food is produced.

Second, the benefits of fresh fruits and vegetables far outweigh the risk of any carcinogens in your food. I am not making this up. Dr. Bruce Ames, of UC Berkeley- of all places, did the research years ago. Ames is quoted as saying, "I think pesticides lower the cancer rate" (Brody). His point is that the benefit of fruits and vegetables in our diet far outweigh the risk from pesticides. Ames notes there are

31

more naturally occurring carcinogens in a cup of coffee or tea than there are synthetic pesticides in our foods:

A cup of coffee is filled with chemicals. They've identified a thousand chemicals in a cup of coffee. But we only found 22 that have been tested in animal cancer tests out of this thousand. And of those, 17 are carcinogens. There are 10 milligrams of known carcinogens in a cup of coffee and that's more carcinogens than you're likely to get from pesticide residues for a year! (Postrel).

Ames is not an advocate for agriculture. He is a biochemist and his research focuses on cancer.

Diet is at least as important as smoking as a cause of cancer," he said in a tone reminiscent of parents coaxing children to eat their broccoli. "If you don't eat your vegetables, you're irradiating yourself in a sense. (Ames' colleague Dr.) Gladys Block has shown that the rate for practically every type of cancer is doubled among people who don't eat fruits and vegetables. Probably every vitamin in foods is part of some defense system (Brody).

Dr. Ames' research has changed his personal eating habits:

I never smoked, and when I married my Italian wife 34 years ago, I switched my diet from Jewish cooking to Italian cooking and never looked back," he said. "I eat lots of fruits and vegetables and fish, but meat in moderation and few processed foods. We use mainly olive oil, and each day I take 250 milligrams of vitamin C, 400 international units of vitamin E and a one-a-day. I eat a good diet, so the supplements are just for insurance. However, I believe in moderation. I don't think people should take massive doses of vitamins (Brody).

Dr. Ames notes, "Environmentalists are forever issuing scare reports based on very shallow science" (Brody). The fact is that the benefits of eating fresh fruits and vegetables far out weighs the risk of any pesticides in our food supply.

"Dr. Ames considers pesticides an anticancer weapon because their use increases the yield of fruits and vegetables and lowers their cost, enabling more people to consume foods that appear to protect against cancer" (Brody).

One of the issues we have to address is that less than two percent of the U.S. population live and work on farms. With so few people living and working on our farms, we need to make sure this "happy few" have the tools they need to produce the food for the rest of us. Unless a huge portion of the American population is prepared to go back to work on the farm pulling weeds we need modern herbicides. For the record, I don't see this kind of population shift happening. I am one of the few in the last century to leave the city and go back to the farm. My own children have sought their careers outside agriculture.

Not only is migration back to the farm not necessary, it is bad policy. Today, Switzerland, Sweden and Denmark are known as prosperous countries. A little over a century ago they could barely feed themselves. Each country made a conscious choice to move away from subsistence agriculture to commodity production for trade and that was the start of their modern prosperity (Fahrni 53).

Next, if you really want to save the planet you need to consider pesticides. Dennis Avery wrote a book, <u>Saving the Planet with Pesticides and Plastics</u>. That may sound counter-intuitive, but here is Avery's logic; with less pesticides we would have to use more acres to grow our food and how would that affect the planet?

> Pesticides are a vital element of the high-yield farming system which is already saving 10 million square miles from being plowed for food production. By 2050, pesticides and fertilizers could be helping to save from plow-down as much as 30 million square miles of forests, prairies and other prime wildlife habitat (Avery 30-31).

Avery's message is that instead of listening to the Chicken Littles we should consider the benefits of modern agriculture, not just for us as consumers, but also for the environment.

Another reason we do not grow organic is it doesn't work. Avery notes the example of China in the 1960's.

The Lesson Learned in China

China attempted to follow an organic farming system in the 1960's under Mao Tse Tung. Mao wanted to increase food production without investing in fertilizer production or paying for food imports.

Under his direction, the Chinese intensified their traditional efforts to collect all animal manure and night soil [for those who don't know night soil is human waste]. They gathered as much biomass from their hillsides as they could to add mulch to the rice and wheat fields. This organic farming method was implemented with all of the intensity that one of the most coercive regimes in world history could muster and with 600 million pairs of hands. The mjor result of this intensive organic effort was to strip the hillsides of their vegetation, generate a massive increase in soil erosion- and produce an agonizingly small increase in food production.

The FAO Production Yearbooks show the story in stark black and white. Food production per capita rose only 5 percent during the decade of the 1960's, and increased only 1 percent annually during the whole 1960-76 period. By 1970 China offered its consumers only 1,984 calories per day, compared to a developing-country average of 2,103. Much of that (millions of tons of wheat in most years) had to be imported.

China suffered a major famine (30 million deaths) in 1959/60 due to its poor farming policies. By the late 1970s, China still had 200 million malnourished citizens (its own estimate). Grain production per capita virtually stagnated. Soil erosion was on a collision course with population growth.

The Chinese Communist government was shaken to its core by the unrelenting pressure to deliver more grain. The country lacked exports to pay for heavy food imports on a continuing basis.

In 1978, China began one of the most dramatic shifts in agricultural policy the world has ever seen. The first change was a decision to make massive investments in chemical fertilizer. Chinese fertilizer applications which had risen slowly from 4 million tons to 7 million tons in the 1970-77 period, jumped to more than 17 million tons in the following seven years. The second major change was to scrap China's big communal farms and lease its farmland back to families. (Mao was dead by this time; he probably would not have permitted such a radical departure of state farm ownership.)

The result of the two changes was the biggest surge in food production ever seen, anywhere in the world. Grain output soared from 242 million tons in 1976 to 283 million tons in 1980 and 389 million tons in 1990!

Because China increased its grain yields from an average of 2.4 tons per hectare in 1970 to 4.2 tons per hectare in 1990, it produced this massive gain in food without a major increase in grain plantings. China used 88 million hectares for grain in 1970, 104 million acres in 1979, and had cut back its grain plantings to 93 million hectares by 1990 (Avery 178-9).

This is not theory, this is real world fact. Modern organic farming was an experiment tried on an incredibly large scale in China, and it failed. The Chinese Communist government which had the zeal of true believers gave up and shifted over to modern, Western conventional farming methods complete with synthetic fertilizers and private sector production.

The example of Biosphere II

The crew of Boisphere 2 recently emerged from two years in their self-contained ecosystem near Tucson, AZ. They had originally planned to spend half their time raising their own food and the other half on scientific experiments.

They never got the chance to do much science. Insects and plant diseases found their way into the biosphere, and the crew had pledged to fight them without man made chemicals. Mites ate the beans and potatoes. Powdery mildew shriveled the squash. The natural oils which were supposed to control insects attracted cockroaches, which infested the living quarters. The sweet potatoes did well- and the crew ate so many that the beta carotene gave some of them orange-tinted skin. Even though 20 percent of the food they ate had been stored in the biosphere before the mission began (for emergencies) the crew lost about 25 pounds each. Hunger was a constant companion, they reported, dominating their thoughts (Avery 188).

The dreams of another group of true believers crash against the rocks of reality. Farming is hard. Producing food is not a game and the consequences of failure are real. The members of the Biosphere 2 crew were haunted by hunger. Thirty million Chinese died of famine. Remember, the 1998 Nobel Prize for Economics was won by Amartya Sen who won it by proving that governments cause famine though poor policy.

Finally, hope for Africa doesn't appear to lie in organic farming either. Those who dream of solving our food production equation without synthetic fertilizers might want to listen to someone who is on the front line of food production where the stakes are high. Norman Bourlag has written, "Some people say that Africa's food problems can be solved without the application of chemical fertilizers. They're dreaming. It's not possible" (Financial Times). Bourlag is neither a chemical salesman, nor a political flack. He won the Nobel Peace Prize as the Father of the Green Revolution in the 20th Century. He arguably has saved more lives than any person in the history of the world. There are many in the environmental and organic communities that criticize his work. The fact is that his ideas did work and help create food stability for large masses of the human population for the first time of our species.

There is a reason that our ancestors moved away from organic farming as soon as they could apply modern science. Organic farming is not reliable and for some odd reason we like a reliable food supply.

Addressing Fear

The sad irony is that we have the safest, most abundant and affordable food supply in the history of the world and we are scared of our food. Think about it.

Affordable- What percentage of your income do you spend on food? The average American family spends less than 15% of their income on food. The Italians I met said they spend 30-35% of their income on food. OK, their food is fabulous. That is probably a good deal. But, can you imagine if you spent 30-35% of your income on food? The Indians I met in 1996 said they spent 60% of their income on food and they are vegetarians! There would be riots on the streets of America if we had to spend anywhere near 60% of our income on food.

Abundant-In our county there are over three hundred different crops grown. Granted, California's Central Valley is the nation's salad bowl, but we don't eat all that produce ourselves. We have an amazing food system that provides a true cornucopia of farm products. I am amazed at the amount of products grocery stores carry today compared to when I was a kid.

Safe- I was asked in an interview years ago if I thought the food supply was safe. I said, "Of course. Think about it, if one child gets sick on milk it makes national news doesn't it?"

Think about this for a moment- what chemicals do you have under your sink? You have stuff under your sink that I would get fined for using on the farm. That is OK. I don't want to use that stuff on my farm. My point is, this is another case of where we are more comfortable when we have some level of control.

We were in Berkeley for a friend's wedding years ago. There was a reception before the wedding at this nice lady's home. She had a beautiful garden full of fabulous roses. When our hostess found out I was a farmer, she asked me all sorts of questions. The two that stood out were her questions on irrigation and pesticides. I asked her about her garden. I, for one, cannot grow roses without having some aphids right after the first bloom in the Spring. I have tried soaps and tobacco juice to get rid of the aphids. They don't really work for more than a day at a time. So now, I use something a little stronger. Since our hostess had such beautiful roses and she lived in the ecologically-correct People's Republic of Berkeley, I asked her what she used to control the pests in her roses. She hesitated, then admitted she didn't use organic methods. Even in the middle of Berkley she showed the natural preference for results over theory and all she was growing were ornamental roses. How much more important are results when we are talking about our food?

In 1996, I wrote a column titled "Dr. Strange Bug, or how I stopped worrying and learned to love pesticides." In that column I wrote,

> The "fear industrial complex" of professional worriers has done a good job convincing the public that their food is poisoned and all farm chemicals cause cancer. No one stops to think, "If our food is poisoned, then why are we living longer, healthier lives than our ancestors?

I don't want to minimize serious concerns about our food supply. I think farmers must publically and continually demonstrate how we produce your food carefully and safely. But, I also want to put things in perspective. We have an incredible food supply. In fact, instead of the risk of starvation, what is America's food problem right now? We are overeating. Crazy. Not only are we overeating, but we are eating the wrong stuff. Instead of eating fresh fruits and vegetables as recommended by Dr. Ames, we are pigging out on fast food and processed foods. Remember, according to Dr. Ames, from a nutrition stand point, the fast food and junk food we are eating are more risky than any possible pesticides you are going to find in your food.

I will address fear and overall environmental issues more directly in Reason 4 when I talk about our Chicken Little mentality. For the moment, I just want to focus on fear and our food. We have been unnecessarily scared of our food for a long time. In their book, Facts, Not Fear Sanera and Shaw illustrate how fear is being used to indoctrinate our children in our schools. The only antidote for fear is solid facts and information.

Summary

Organic food is fine. If you want to pay a premium for your food, knock yourself out. The fact is our conventionally grown foods are safe and there is strict government oversight on our food supply, as there should be. Remember, often it only takes one case of food poisoning to make national news. We are very careful about our food supply, as we should be. That vigilance must be constant. I am not, for one moment, suggesting we eliminate government oversight. Let's just make sure the regulations are reasonable. Let's stop trying to scare ourselves about our food supply. Dixy Lee Ray was a former governor of the State of Washington and former Chair of the U.S, Atomic Energy Commission. I like what she has to say about modern agriculture.

"Sometimes in the future, when the accomplishments of the 20th century are recorded for posterity, it may finally be acknowledged that our greatest achievement by far has been the introduction of high-tech, high-yield agriculture. Measured in terms of benefit to human society, an adequate diet of nutritious, abundant, and affordable food eclipses all other developments of this most remarkable century. Neither computer technology nor transistors, robotics, advances in communication and transportation, life-saving antibiotics and modern medicine, nuclear energy, synthetics, plastics and the entire petro-chemical industry rank as high in importance as the advances in food production. And all these other wonderful breakthroughs probably could not have happened *without* a well fed population" (Ray 67).

Amen.

Reason Seven:

Solutions

#7-I'll start believing environmentalists when they start offering solutions. What I usually see is a presentation of a problem and then they jump up and down and tell us to stop it. For example, they will tell us how bad over population is. Then tell us to stop it. What kind of solution is that? It would be nice if the solutions made sense. One suggestion they had about dust on dirt roads in our area was to water the dirt roads every day. Do you know how many miles of dirt roads there are in Fresno County? Do you know how much water that would take? Do you know how many of those roads have no traffic at all during the day? That wasn't much of solution. Watering the roads we use makes a lot more sense. But, the farmers had to suggest that, the enviros didn't figure that one out.

My experience working with the environmental community is they are not interested in problem solving.

As I shared earlier, my introduction to the environmental community was a Sierra Club meeting in San Diego when I was sixteen. [Please remember, this was years before I started farming.] The sum of the meeting was as follows, "Well, we beat the nuclear guys on that issue, who do we go after next?" I never found out what issue they beat the nuclear guys on. The whole point of the meeting was, "where is our next victim?" Even as a starry-eyed idealist, ready to enlist in the cause I was repulsed by this approach, and I was out of there. I will gladly work for a cause I believe in, but I don't go around picking fights to throw my weight around.

Another experience was working with a Bay Area environmental group. In a side bar conversation I tried to engage David Behar of the Bay Institute about how to solve water supply problems to benefit both the environment and the farmers. Behar's comment was, "This is a Zero-Sum game." He felt that if one side wins the other side must lose. Can you see how this perspective automatically limits our ability to solve problems? Right off the bat he has eliminated one of the most powerful tools for solving problems; The Win-Win. Or, as Fisher, Ury and Patton put it in their classic, Getting to Yes!, "Seek Options for Mutual Gain" (Fisher and Ury 56). This experience confirmed once again that the enviros not only do not want to "Seek options for mutual gain", in my experience they are not interested in problem solving at all. To me, that is not a reasonable approach to the issues we face.

In Reason Three I share my experience on a Technical Advisory Committee for the Central Valley Regional Water Quality Control Board. Each of the technical experts on the committee was locked into his or her specialty. The salt guys didn't want to consider any solutions until the salt issue was solved. The fertilizer guys didn't want to consider any solutions until all the fertilizer issues were solved. I think you get the idea. We were gridlocked because each side was focused only on their issue and their problem. They had neither perspective on the larger picture, nor any desire to address anyone else's problem until their problem was resolved. Again, this is not a reasonable approach to the problems we face.

The Enviros Have No Responsibility to Produce Anything

Another reason I think we see a lack of solutions from the enviros is they don't have any responsibility to produce anything. When your prime directive is to protect the environment, at all costs, everything else can fall to the way side.

You and I have to produce something or provide a service to support our families. All the things we have in our lives do not magically appear. For example, the coffee you drank this morning came from beans grown overseas. They had to be nurtured, harvested, roasted, ground and shipped thousands of miles to get to your home. All of this does not happen by magic or by accident. It takes a lot of work, a lot of planning, a lot of effort and that is just for one cup of coffee. How about the rest of the food you ate today? Or, the clothes you wear. [I, for one, would love to visit half the places my clothes have been to. But again, that is another issue.]

My point is that producing the mere necessities of our lives takes a lot of work. [It is a fairly fragile system. Consider what happens when war or a hurricane disrupts the system.] Our environmental friends and neighbors feel zero responsibility in the production of the necessities of life. Their over-riding primary goal is protection of the environment. It is a noble goal, but it lacks balance.

In Reason Four I discuss how the enviros use the Precautionary Principle to shut down productivity and progress. At first the Precautionary Principle sounds like a good idea, we will not do anything until we prove it will do no harm. But, if our prime directive was to avoid all risk, we could not get out of bed in the morning.

You Can't Politicize Everything

Liberals tend to politicize everything. Yes, I know it's politics and conservatives politicize things too. But, I think the Liberals go farther. For example, look at the 2008 Presidential Campaign. Then candidate Obama promised his daughters a dog if he won the election. He even mentioned the promise during his acceptance speech on election night. That began a national discussion on what kind of dog the Obamas should get. Who drove that debate? It wasn't the conservatives. The Liberals made this an issue. The dog couldn't be a pure bred because that was elitist and it supported puppy mills. Should it be a rescue dog? A mixed breed was an issue since one of the Obama girls has allergies and pure breds are more hypo-allergenic. Pu-leez. This was a promise from a Dad to his daughters. I don't care what kind of dog they get. The Liberals made an issue out of something that should be off limits. Even the Mafia leaves your family alone.

The reason I bring up the penchant for politicizing everything is that it clouds judgment. This does cut both ways. Both sides try ramming their ideological square pegs through Reality's round holes.

I get it. Politics is a passionate sport. But, you have to be able to pull back from the immediate passion and look at the bigger picture. The things voters are concerned about are often not the things politicians and special interests are interested about. Voters are concerned about good public policy not power politics. What politicians forget is good policy is good politics. Where are the statesmen in politics today? They get drowned out by the extremists on both ends. Grenade throwers make better sound bites than reasoned debate. The public doesn't care who's in office. They care about things like well maintained roads to go to work on, safe neighborhoods, good schools for their kids, safe food and water. When we lose focus good public policy gets lost in the political shuffle.

Correlation and Causation

I don't know if my grad school advisor will be embarrassed that I bring this up or happy I remember something from class. The first rule in the social sciences is "correlation does not equal causation." That is a mouthful, but it is important. We cannot have good solutions unless we are clear on this principle. There are a lot of bad ideas floating around out there because people have neglected this principle. Here are two examples, from my experience, in our region.

Air Quality

Ten years ago, health advocates in our area noticed the increase in childhood asthma and the fact that we live in an agricultural region. They took those two facts and started advocating for stricter air rules on agriculture because they "knew" that childhood asthma, in our area, was caused by dust from farming. Ironically, at the same time a study came out from the British medical journal The Lancet, showing that European farm kids had lower incidences of asthma than their city neighbors (Lancet). How could that be? The conclusion the Brits came to was asthma is an indoor disease. Modern kids are spending more time indoors watching TV and playing video games than they used to. In the closed environment of a home there are more allergens to trigger asthma than even the dust and dirt of a farm. This is not a fluke. The Lancet study was followed by a study reported in the April 2012 Journal of Allergy and Clinical Immunology showing that Amish farm children in the American Mid West have even lower incidences of asthma than children on Swiss farms (Holbreich). The conclusion that asthma is caused by farm dust is not supported by science.

I took this information to public meetings and the health advocates blew me off. Their preconceptions and their politics blinded them to the reality staring them in the face. [Years later the Lung Association changed their practice, if not their policy. Now they will come to your house, do a survey for allergens and give you tips on how to clean your home from allergens.] This is just one example of what happens when are not clear about correlation and causation. Yes, childhood asthma was increasing. Yes, we are in farm country. But, that doesn't mean there is a causal link. If asthma is an indoor disease, you can control all the dust on every farm and it still won't cure the childhood asthma problem.

Another Example: Food Policy

The latest Crisis du Jour is the obesity epidemic. Yes, this is a serious issue. The "du Jour" part is that advocates have watched our waist lines expand and they have seen the increase of fast food and convenience stores. They have also seen the loss of small, neighborhood grocery stores as they have been replaced by large chain stores. Their conclusion? We need more neighborhood grocery stores selling fruits and vegetables. Huh? I understand and support the idea of more fruits and vegetables in our diets. I personally am always looking for new foods and new recipes to increase my consumption of fruits and veggies. [I really wish fresh strawberry margaritas counted as a serving of fresh fruit.] But, putting more grocery stores in these 'food deserts' won't solve the problem. Many people made fun of Nancy Reagan's "Just Say No" anti-drug slogan; how is this any different? It's not going to change the fundamental problem. If we change demand the market will follow. The issue right now is that cheese burgers taste better than tofu and potato chips taste better than celery sticks. The LA Times reported a story showing, "Better access to supermarkets –long touted as a way to curb obesity in low income neighborhoods- doesn't improve people's diets, according to research...which tracked thousands of people for over 15 years" (Hernandez).

Even with this study, my food advocate friends try to argue that access to fruits and veggies is the issue and if we just had more farmers markets everything would be fine. This is a two-fer: their political preconceptions blind them from seeing the problem clearly and their inability to see the difference between correlation and causation interfere with their ability to develop good public policy.

The Importance of Good Public Policy

Good public policy is good politics, and the stakes in good public policy are high. We think famines are caused by bad weather like droughts. The 1998 Nobel Prize in Economics was won by Amartya Sen for proving it is government policy that causes famine, not bad weather. If government policy can starve people to death, a slow and excruciating way to go, we should be concerned about good policy.

Politics is About Good Policy, Not Compromise

We often hear politics is the "art of compromise." Really? How do you feel when you have to compromise? Don't you feel shorted because you had to give something up? Compromise as a method creates strange political Kabuki. You have to ask for a full loaf, knowing you will only get half a loaf. Why not ask for the half loaf you really want? In public negotiations, I was literally told that asking for what you really want is bargaining in bad faith. What? When being honest is considered bargaining in bad faith, we should know something is wrong.

There is an alternative to compromise. I teach critical thinking and problem solving. One of the methods I teach is interest based negotiation. [I am highly indebted to and I highly recommend Fisher, Ury and Patton's <u>Getting to Yes!</u>] The best illustration of interest based negotiation is the story of two boys and one orange. Two boys come to Mom fighting over an orange. Mom is busy, she cuts the orange in half and gives each son one half. Problem solved. One son takes his half, scoops out the fruit to eat and throws the rind away. The other son takes his half, scoops out the fruit, throws the fruit away and keeps the rind for an art project. I know Moms are busy, but if this Mom had taken a moment to ask what each son wanted, they both could have had all of what they wanted (Fisher and Ury 56f).

Finding Solutions

Sorting out the needs in public policy is one of the main functions of leadership. Sadly, we have too few statesmen who lead in this manner. The special interests, are by definition, focused on their issue, usually to the exclusions of all others. [We will look at one dimensional problem solving in Reason Three- Seeing the Big Picture.] The more common approach is the full-contact approach that demands compromise and concession. People leave with half a loaf feeling they have been compromised, they have been taken advantage of. All of this interferes with finding solutions to the serious environmental problems in the world today.

Yes, politics are important, but we should not politicize everything- that blinds us.

Good policy is good politics. Good policy, making the right decisions for the community in the long run, is good politics. We have too many politicians that are looking only at the next election cycle.

There are alternatives to compromise. Methods like interest based negotiations take time, but they can create better solutions in the long run.

The stakes are high. If bad government policy can starve people to death then we want to get this right.

I would hope the end goal is solving problems, not winning arguments. I realize I am a raving idealist. But, there is a fundamental difference between solving problems and winning arguments.

Think about it. At home with your family, is it better to solve a problem or win an argument? Gentlemen, you may feel the momentary satisfaction of winning an argument with your wife, how does that work for you in the long run? Parents, you can pull rank and win an argument with a teenager, how does that work down the road? Problem solving is hard.

Problem solving takes hard work and the reality for many in public policy is that we are in the middle of what political consultant Ed Rollins called bare knuckle brawls. My own experience in politics is that statement can be true. When you are working to win an election it is an all out fight. The problem today is that politicians are in constant election mode. The need for campaign funds keeps them constantly focused on the next election. Being in campaign mode, all the time, does not allow them the opportunity to step back from a public policy issue and look at the long term perspective. Special interests from all sides are on them for solutions- now! Remember, we live in a society where instant coffee is too slow. But, creating solutions usually takes time.

My experience is that environmentalists are not really interested in problem solving. They don't do their own bench science. They are more interested in lawsuits and regulations than figuring out the technical solutions to the problems we face. Consider the national CAFE, Corporate Average Fuel Economy Standards. While I have been writing this chapter [July 2011] the Federal Government raised CAFE standards again. No one in the government is going to do any research to help raise automobile mileage. No one in the environmental community is going to raise a finger to do a moment's research to raise mileage. They just wave their magic wands and declare that mileage should be raised. This is a ridiculous method of problem solving.

Reason Six:

Crisis du Jour

#6-Crisis du Jour: When was the last time you heard about the ozone layer or the rainforest? Remember when that was all we heard about? Did the problem go away? Did it get solved? I'll start believing the environmentalists when they stick with an issue until it is solved not skip from one issue to the next depending on their Hollywood celebrity or rock concert.

I think there is an unholy alliance between politicians and environmental groups. Each feeds off the other. Careers are built on these issues. Look at Al Gore. Would we have heard anything from him since he left the Vice Presidency if it weren't for his environmental crusade? If I understand correctly a biologist can make a career by being the world's lone expert of a threatened species. Fundraising for environmental groups is easier when they have a pending crisis.

I am not saying these are bad people. As a student of ethics I am pointing out that there are built in conflicts of interest that we should be aware of.

Invisible Crises

The current Crisis du Jour is global climate change. (It began as global warming, someone realized they couldn't make that case and they changed gears. This too raises questions.)

Do you want me to be as environmentally sound as possible? Excellent. I am in. Do you want me to upend the economy on what you have told me so far? I don't think so. Have you noticed the current crusades are invisible? In the 60's and 70's it was easy to rally support for environmental causes; there was smoke in the air, rivers were so full of garbage they caught on fire and there were pictures of endangered species like baby seals. Since then, it has been harder to 'see' the problem. The Endangered Species Act is used to protect dung beetles, not Bambi. Who could see the ozone layer? And, now you want me to change everything because a computer model says the Earth's temp may go up two degrees Fahrenheit fifty years after I am dead? Can you at least understand why I might be a little skeptical?

A Lack of Perspective

George Santayana is famously quoted as reminding us, "those who neglect history are bound to repeat it" (Zhao 26). This is a true and an important reason to study history. I think there is an even more important reason to study history- it gives us perspective.

The 24 hour news cycle and the rush of daily life keep us pretty well focused on the moment. The problem of living in the moment is that we have no perspective. When I teach U. S. history I start by asking my students, what are the top issues of today? The usual answers involve things like immigration, racism, sexism the environment and the economy. I take and show them how each of their issues ties back to our history. Immigration? This isn't the first time we have had concerns about immigrants coming to the U.S. and impacting our economy and our culture. The environment? These concerns go back to the Industrial Revolution, but really took on new energy after WWII. My point is that Solomon was right, there is "nothing new under the sun" (Ecclesiastes 1:9). An understanding of history gives us a perspective on the issues before us. With perspective we are less likely to flicker from one crisis to the next.

Consider the example of the great environmental causes of the last thirty years. Do you remember when the ozone hole was continual front page news like climate change is now? There was endless chatter and hand wringing. The ozone hole was a man made disaster that was going to crispy critter us all if it wasn't solve immediately by massive legislation. Why don't we hear about the ozone hole anymore? Sure, a few laws were passed. CFC production was limited. Air conditioning coolant was changed – and made much more expensive. But, I don't remember getting the memo that we fixed the ozone hole.

Another Crisis du Jour was the rain forest. Do you remember that one? Rock stars held concerts. Congress held hearings. We even have a chain of restaurants now. Someone came up with a deal where you could buy an acre of rain forest to protect it from development. [Actually, now we are on to something. Private property rights are a powerful tool not only to protect our freedom but to also protect the environment. Garrett Hardin had it wrong. The real Tragedy of the Commons is that what ever is owned by all is cared for by none. Be honest, which would you rather use, the restroom at a public park or the restroom at a privately owned business? Yep, me too. I'll write more about this in the final chapter. Meanwhile, back to the rain forest.]

What did all the rock concerts and Congressional hearings accomplish? Sure, some areas were protected as parks, but we didn't lower consumer demand of anything which is the real cause creating pressure to convert rain forest to commercial production.[Another thing that gets me is rock stars holding concerts to encourage us to donate money to the environment or any other of their causes. Let's get serious, if the goal is to buy rain forest land and protect it from development those rock stars can dig more money out of their sofa cushions than you and I can donate.]

Do you see my point though? What makes climate change any different from the ozone hole or the rain forest?

The Problem When Science and Politics Meet

In 2004, Michael Crichton published a novel titled <u>State of Fear</u>. It is the first novel I have ever read that had footnotes and graphs. In the novel, Crichton uses the Crisis du Jour of global climate change to take on the issue of how we have politicized science. In fact, at the end of his novel there is an appendix titled, "Why Politicized Science is Dangerous." [When have you ever seen a novel with an appendix?] In his summary Crichton quotes Alston Chase, "when the search for truth is confused with political advocacy, the pursuit of knowledge is reduced to the quest for power" (Crichton 580). Crichton's pitch is for publically supported pure research, which is a nice dream, but unrealistic. His point is, without a separation of science and politics all sorts of bad things can happen and Truth is the first thing to get lost in the shuffle.

The point in Crichton's novel is that the unholy alliance of science and politics in this case has created a state of fear that is not grounded in reality. Remember, Crichton was trained in science, he graduated Harvard Medical School and earned an M.D.. Crichton accepts that "Atmospheric carbon dioxide is increasing and human activity is the probable cause" (Crichton 569). But, he puts the climate within a greater perspective. "We are also in the midst of a natural warming trend that began about 1850, as we emerged from a four hundred year cold spell known as the "Little Ice Age"" (Crichton 569). Here, again, is an illustration of the importance of putting the latest Crisis du Jour in perspective. Climate change is not about this summer's heat or last winter's blizzards. That is current news. Climate change is not even about what has happened since the beginning of the Industrial Revolution. The last hundred and eighty years are important, but even that is too small a window of time. What is the climate cycle over the last ten thousand years? The last hundred thousand years? The last million years?

Crichton has one of his characters say, "for the last seven hundred years, our planet has been in a geological ice age, characterized by advancing and retreating glacial ice" (563). I know at this point some of you are thinking, "Hey, you are quoting characters in a novel, that's not a legitimate source of information." You have a point, but please remember there is a tradition in American literature of novels changing the public debate. Remember Uncle Tom's Cabin? More importantly, remember when I said this is the first novel I have read with footnotes and graphs? On pages 193 and 194 Crichton has a series of footnotes backing his assertion that Antarctica is cooling, not melting as many fear. His references are not from hack political journals. Crichton cites Science, Nature, Geology, Geophysical Research Letters, the Annals of Glaciology and the Journal of Climate. My point is that if we can gain a little perspective on the problem, I think we will be better at developing solutions to what present themselves as Crises du Jour.

Reason Five:

Public Education

#5- I'll start believing environmentalists when they start doing effective public education. After nearly 40 years they have failed to develop effective environmental awareness. People say they are environmentalists then they drive big SUV's. There is a disconnect.

Public education is slow and tedious work. But, as Emile Durkhiem said a century ago-"When people are moral no laws are necessary. When people are not moral no law are sufficient." The point is that when we have a well developed public awareness about the environment we would need endless laws and endless debates to scare us into compliance.

You could say we have been doing public education for a generation now. I would say it is *'public education lite': feels great, less helpful*. We are barely making a dent in personal choices. We can make people feel guilty about the environment. We can make them tell politicians to fix the environment. We can all agree that someone else is responsible- the great "them". What we are not getting through to people is how our personal choices make a difference. You can go into Starbucks, have a great conversation about how we need to care for the environment and then everyone tosses their one use paper cups in the trash as they go out the door.

Recently I was teaching a class in Critical Thinking and Problem Solving. The assignment included responding to a report on whether or not to drill for oil. Each student agreed drilling for oil is too risky for the environment, but not one addressed what they were doing to lower fossil fuel consumption. They are intelligent, caring students. They just couldn't make the connection.

Why is the idea of making connection so important? We are not just talking about a theory. We are talking about caring for our habitat. If there is a real threat, then we need to address that threat in practice, not just in theory. Why am I pushing so hard for personal involvement in the issue? Because, if our lifestyles are a threat to the environment, then we need to address our lifestyles. We cannot just pawn this problem off on to someone else's shoulders.

I have a lot of respect for Gandhi. He was one of the great souls of the 20th Century. As long as we study history we will read of his personal commitment to peace. One of the nearly forgotten stories of Gandhi's life is that during the Boer War, at the end of the 19th Century, he set up an ambulance corps for the British. He and his men would go up to the battle lines and take wounded soldiers back to receive aid. Clearly, they were non-combatants. But, Gandhi admitted that he and they were part of the British War effort even though they were pacifists (Gandhi 214). There is an honesty in what Gandhi said about what he and his men did. We need a similar honesty about environmental issues. It is too easy for us to blame others for the environmental problems we face. It is too easy to pass off responsibility to someone else. Even if you drive a hybrid car, you are still using fossil fuel. It may be less fuel, but it is still fossil fuel. If you go buy an all-electric car, one environmentalist reminds us, that your electric car is only as clean as your source of electricity. If you are buying electricity from a coal-fired plant, what have you achieved? Except for the rare individual living in a shack, raising their own food and living entirely off the grid, we are all in this together. There is no "us" and "them. We surely all have a stake on seeing these problems solved. Real public education on environmental issues must make the connection between the environment and our personal choices.

One of my professors in grad school was a self-defined radical environmentalist. The class I took from him was on international environmental policy. He and I locked horns a few times and I was worried I would be flunked out of the class. I will give him credit, as passionately as he believes in his cause and as fundamentally as we disagreed on the issues, he respected my point of view and I passed the class.

One conversation I had with him was enlightening. I challenged him with a question- Why does the environmental community rely on legislation and lawsuits instead of doing the research to find solutions to environmental problems? Legislation and lawsuits don't help me learn to farm greener and better. His response was interesting, "Business people are innovators. You will figure it out." Wow. So their job is to move the goal posts and my job is to figure out how to get there. Does that seem fair to you? Do you see what I mean, when I say, we do not have effective public education on the environment? They aren't even trying. Maybe it is too hard. Going to the state capitol or to DC is more fun than sitting in a lab or being out in the field wrestling with complex problems. I am sure the high moral ground feels better, but these problems will not solve themselves. The batteries on my magic wand wore out years ago. We need really smart people out in the field with us trying to figure out things like natural sources of bug control, not sitting in court rooms or legislative offices trying to figure ways to penalize me if I don't figure out how.

Addressing Fear

Americans are generally scared of nuclear power. That fear was re-ignited by the earthquake and tsunami in Japan that triggered a nuclear crisis in March, 2011. The French get somewhere between sixty and eighty percent of their electricity from nuclear power. They don't seem to be scared of nuclear power. Do you know why? Dr. Robert DuPont, a researcher as Georgetown University, says the French nuclear power plants are open for public tours. In fact, the French encourage school groups to visit nuclear power plants. Familiarity encourages understanding. Du Pont says the visits make the nuclear power plants, "familiar with people…so that vaccinates the people, it immunizes them from fear once it is familiar" (NPR 22 March 2011).

Fear is *the* driving emotion in our discussions on the environment. Fear as a negative force is a more powerful motivator in our public dialogue on the environment than the positive emotion of care-giving for the environment. We are more scared of being hurt or hurting the environment than we are driven to care for the natural world. I think we will be better off when we get beyond fear to a positive care for the environment. Don't we all prefer when religious people are motivated by the love of God than those who are motivated by judgment? There is a parallel here.

Fear is a poor motivator for positive action. John Stossel, the journalist, raised the question, "Are we scaring ourselves to death?" On top of scaring ourselves to death we seem to be scaring ourselves into inaction. The problems seem too big for any of us to deal with individually. Eventually, I think, we tune the problem out and go on with our lives, and leave the problems to someone else.

Why Fear Doesn't Help

There are a number of reasons why fear doesn't help in our public dialogue on environmental issues. I want to focus on two of these reasons-

First, fear drives us to non-rational decisions.

Second, fear distracts us from the real issues.

These are similar reasons, but they are worth separating out.

In a 2007 *Psychology Today* article titled, "Ten Ways We Get the Odds Wrong", the authors highlight how we fear the wrong things. Because of ancestral memory, we are wired to fear snakes more than we fear cars (Psychology Today). But, more people in the U.S. will die in car wrecks this year than will die of snake bite. Fear drives us to non- rational decisions. This is merely ironic when we are talking about cars and snakes. But, when fear drives public policy and we make wrong choices, there can be serious consequences.

Twenty years ago Meryl Streep used her Hollywood celebrity and had us washing our fruits and vegetables with soap and water because she was concerned about the possibility of pesticides in our foods. She led a protest to ban a fungicide used in apples. The result was the collapse of apple production in Washington State.

What did Ms. Streep accomplish? Now, we import a lot of apples and a lot of apple juice from China which has less regulation and oversight than we have here. Families lost their farms. People lost their jobs. And, we are no safer than we were before. Fear drove us to make non-rational decisions.

Dr. Bruce Ames, a researcher at UC-Berkeley, writes that the benefits from eating fruits and vegetables far out weight the risk of pesticides in our foods. This is another example of how fear not only causes us to make non-rational choices, it also distracts us from real issues. Of course the safe use of farm chemicals is important. But, the real issue is how public health is served by a healthy diet which includes fruits and vegetables.

Emile Durkheim, the father of modern sociology, is quoted as saying, "If people are moral, then no laws are necessary. If people are not moral, no laws are sufficient" (Covey). The modern corollary would be, *"If people care for the environment then no laws will be necessary- we will make the right choices. If we do not make the connection between our actions and the environment no amount of laws will be sufficient."* I suspect if we polled any room full of people in the U.S. they would say they are environmentalists. My question is, how much does this belief affect their lifestyle choices? The choices we make reflect our real moral and ethical positions.

Most people are busy caring for their families and busy at work. They are not crusaders. If they are community minded, they help at their kids' school or coach a baseball team. And that is fine.

Instead of doing the hard work of public education the enviros are lobbying legislators and filing lawsuits. Instead of doing the heavy duty research that actually solve difficult technical problems, they hold marches and rallies.

Do you think I am exaggerating? Consider this- in the wake of the BP oil spill in 2010, did U.S. oil consumption go down? No. A lot of people were concerned about what might happen. The environmental Chicken Littles ran around predicting doom and gloom. But, oil consumption only went down in 2011 due to increased prices at the pump which were caused by other factors.

In the wake of the tsunami-caused problems at the Dai-Ichi Fukushima nuclear power plant in 2011, did electricity consumption go down? No.

It is not that people don't care about the environment, it is they just haven't been taught to connect the dots between their lifestyles and the environment.

Environmental Cynicism

Elsewhere, I bring up the old fable about Chicken Little. Perhaps, this is the place to bring up the story of the Boy Who Cried Wolf. In that story, the little boy got a lot of attention from the village elders when he said he saw a wolf. Not too long ago, wolves were seen as dangerous predators of humans and livestock, not cuddly little plush toys. Wolves were a threat to the community and the elders appreciated the warning, until they realized the little boy hadn't seen a wolf, he just liked the attention. The story ends badly for the little boy. One day, there really is a wolf, but the little boy had lost his credibility with all his false calls. The elders didn't believe him anymore and the wolf ate the little boy.

Sadly, in a very real way I think social activists, today, have squandered a lot of their credibility just like the boy who cried wolf. Let's consider a non-environmental example. Remember in the 1980's how activists lectured us on how bad eggs, butter and red meat were for us? It took years, but it was finally determined that eggs, butter and red meat, in moderation, were part of a healthy diet. Kind of makes you wonder about modern food crusades doesn't it?

Again, let's look at another 80's crusade-the hole in the ozone layer. Millions were spent in research. Rock stars held concerts. Congress held hearings. Laws were passed. Did I miss a memo? I honestly don't remember hearing that we solved the ozone hole problem. [I don't know if we really can 'solve' the ozone hole problem.] It seems that the concern about the ozone hole just kind of ran its course.

My point is that an endless parade of Crises du Jour breed a kind of cynicism. One environmental group or another brings up an issue, people roll their eyes and think, "Here we go again."

I think Durkheim was right, "when people are moral no laws are necessary and when people are not moral then no laws are sufficient." When we can show people a direct connection between their actions and the environment, we won't need more environmental laws, people will make the right choices. Unfortunately we are not making that connection. REDUCE RECYCLE REUSE is a mantra of the environmental community. Look around. When you go to the grocery store, how many people are using reusable bags? In our town, I am 'the guy with his own bags.' When I started using cloth bags years ago, the baggers would put my groceries in a plastic bag and then put it in my cloth bag. Kind of misses the point doesn't it?

How many people are using reusable mugs at Starbucks? I am usually the only one I see when I go there.

Let's Consider Starbucks for a Moment

Starbucks has been tooting their own horn for a long time about how ethical and environmental a company they are. In his 2011 book, <u>Onward</u>, Starbucks CEO Howard Shultz goes on and on about how ethical they are. Let's take a closer look. In terms of being an ethical company, his two claims are employees have health care and they ethically source their coffee. Very cool. Health care? Check. Let's look at the ethical sourcing of their coffee. By their own numbers Shultz's goal is "to ethically source 100% of Starbuck's coffee by 2015, 45% more that we are currently procuring" (Shultz 204). Did you catch that? For forty years they have been tooting their own horn about ethically sourced coffee and they won't reach that goal until 2015? And, in 2015 it will be 100% higher than today? They aren't even close now, after forty years of trying? By their own numbers, Fair Trade coffee only reached 10% of Starbuck's use by 2009 (Shultz 204). Back to the cups- Starbucks serves well over sixty million cups of coffee a week. Until 2010 they didn't even have a plan to recycle <u>one</u> of those sixty million cups (Shultz 324). Sixty million cups is a lot of garbage, especially for a company that makes the environmental claims Starbucks makes.

I don't mean to be a Starbucks basher. My point is, even for a company as successful, as wealthy and as committed as Starbucks is, environmental stewardship is not easy. Until 2010 Starbucks hadn't solved the difficult technical problem of how to recycle their paper cups. The problem is two-fold. USDA limits the amount of recycled paper in food containers for food safety. Also, to make the cups water, or coffee-proof they are poly coated which makes them difficult to recycle. We face difficult technical problems that will require more problem solving than protest marches.

Public Education is Hard

There is no doubt public education on environmental issues is hard, but if we are going to properly care for the environment we must make the connection between the environment and our personal lives. The alternative is unthinkable. We would be left micro-managing people's lives. (Of course, many of us farmers think we are getting micromanaged by regulations already.

How do we help people become more environmentally moral???

The Problem with the Top-Down Approach

Ten years ago, we went through another round of the air wars in our region. A local state senator was trying to make a name for himself and air quality was the issue he was going to use. Hearings were held. It was determined that farmers hadn't done their part to reduce air pollution and by golly they were going to be brought to heel. The reason farmers were resistant was two-fold. We knew we weren't the problem. The vast majority of the air pollution in our valley, according to the state and local air agencies, was caused by vehicular traffic, not by farmers. Secondly, some of the solutions the government wanted to mandate were ridiculous. My personal favorite was the suggestion that we water every dirt road, on every farm in the county, every day. Do you know how much water that would waste? Do you understand that not every dirt road in the county is used every day? Eventually, we worked out rules we could live with, but it took a lot of effort, and it created a lot of cynicism. The politicians and the agency people didn't look like they knew what they were talking about. (Make a note, before you ask people to change their lives you better get your homework right.)

Another Irony-The Issue of Materialism

A couple of years ago, I noticed another irony. They don't talk together often, but the religious community and the environmental community share a common criticism of modern culture- materialism. The medieval church was highly critical of the Renaissance and the Enlightenment. While possible loss of the church's power and influence were factors, the heart of their criticism was materialism; in this case, focus on earthly things would take people's minds away from spiritual things. (For the record- I think we can say, with the confidence of a few centuries of observation, the church fathers were right about this. We are much more materialistic and much less spiritual than our ancestors.)

The modern environmental movement is concerned about materialism for a different reason. Modern materialism equates happiness with the amount of stuff we have. The problem is that creating all this stuff is kind of hard on the planet. (I have to side with the enviros on this one. When I defend the virtues of modern life, I am defending decent food, housing and medical care, not the modern consumer lifestyle. Life has never been about "whoever has the most toys, wins.")

The modern environmental movement and the faith community have long been a little hesitant about each other. Most participants in Earth Day celebrations and weekend clean ups don't know the history of this tension.

It has been suggested that Lynn White's 1976 essay in Science was a wedge between the environmental and religious communities. Perhaps.

White's point was that the environmental problems that welled up in the 60's were the result of the dominant thinking, of the day, which placed humanity outside and superior to the natural world. Since Christianity was the foundation of Western thought, it therefore, bore "a huge burden of guilt" (White).

That kind of statement is the kind of thing that could drive a wedge between two communities. To his credit, White doesn't stop there. White continues, "we shall continue to have a worsening ecological crisis until we reject the Christian axiom that nature has no reason for existence save to serve man" (White). White concludes his essay by proposing St. Francis as "patron saint for ecologists" (White). White says St. Francis is the greatest radical in Christian history since Christ (White). For White, "the key to understanding Francis is his belief in the virtue of humility- not merely for the individual but for man as a species" (White). I agree with White. I don't think the natural world was given to humanity to serve us. As a Christian, I reject what White calls the Christian axiom, I think the mandate of Genesis has been misinterpreted. In the Book of Genesis we were not given license to rape and pillage the environment. We were given the role of caretaker. As a farmer, I use modern technology, but I cannot produce a crop by romping over nature. I must work in harmony with nature to be productive and make a living. There are other Christian writers who have tried to make the same point. Sadly, they are largely ignored in both by the church and the environmental community. [I have listed some of these writers' works in the back.]

For different reasons the environmental movement and the faith communities share a common criticism of modern life- the issue of consumerism. Part of public education should include the issue of consumerism. The enviros are concerned that modern consumerism is not good for the planet. The faith community is concerned it is not good for the soul.

The symbol for me of American consumerism having gone over the top is not the bling, a three car garage or a summer cabin. For me, the symbol of consumerism gone awry is a plastic, light saber spoon that was a free 'prize' in a box of breakfast cereal. Since, I don't eat breakfast cereal often, I don't know how I ended up with two spoons, much less one. When I was a kid, getting a prize in a box of cereal or Cracker Jacks was a big deal. But, this spoon is no magic decoder ring. It has a light, a battery and a switch. This is way over the top. What does it say about out society when a disposable toy has a toxic battery in it.

I believe in freedom. I think free market capitalism is the most productive economic system in human history. I am grateful to be alive in the 21st Century. But, I am pretty sure we missed at least one turn along the way. If you think I am wrong, please take about fifteen minutes to watch one of the "reality" shows on TV. How much of your life matches "reality", as portrayed on TV? How much of your life would you like to match reality TV? I'll pass, thanks anyways.

"A battle to fight and an adventure to live"

In his book, "Wild at Heart", John Eldridge writes, "in the heart of every man is a desperate desire for a battle to fight, an adventure to live and a beauty to win" (Eldridge, John 9). He adds, "I want you to think of the films men love, the things they do with their free time, and especially the aspirations of little boys and see if I am not right on this" (Eldridge, John 9). Eldridge's wife Stasi, writes there are three things a woman's heart longs for, "to be romanced, to play an irreplaceable role in a great adventure, and to unveil beauty" (Eldridge, Stasi 8). Do you see the common thread? Men and women want "an adventure to live" and to "play an irreplaceable role in a great adventure." The battle for the environment can fit into that deep desire for both men and women.

I think the Eldridges are on to something. I know my generation was programmed to save the world. I think we all like being part of something larger than ourselves. Let's consider my nephew. My nephew, Hunter, is a great kid. The family was up for our daughter's wedding. Hunter has a Sea Shepherd sticker on his laptop computer and he comes down one morning with his Sea Shepherd t-shirt on. So, I asked him about the Sea Shepherds. Fortunately their show was on TV and we watched a couple of episodes. Wow, that was fun. The environmental warriors chased the whaling bad guys all over the ocean. They had tactics and strategy. There was drama. There was righteous indignation. What fun. Who wouldn't want to be part of a cause like that?

My problem is that something like that has no impact on our personal lives. My radical environmentalist grad school professor said we will all have to make sacrifices if we are going to save the environment. There is a huge disconnect when Americans criticize people for hunting whales. The end of whale hunting will have virtually no impact on American culture or the American economy. I am fairly confident no one in our family has ever eaten whale meat. Most of the people who watch and support the Sea Shepherds have no personal stake in the issue. Essentially, we are telling other people how they should live. One of the things I was thinking while watching the show was, what about multicultural tolerance? The Japanese who are doing the whaling are a nation that has lived on and near the sea since time immemorial. Sea food and whaling are part of their heritage. I thought one of the values of today's liberals was tolerance and respect for the people and values of other cultures. I guess there are limits to tolerance. When I teach ethics, we define an ethical dilemma as two good, opposing ethical values. Here we have multiculturalism and environmentalism, which value wins out? We are back to the notion of environmentalists as religious busy-bodies.

They key part of public education is that we need to make environmental ethics personal. We need to stop worrying about "them" and start thinking about what <u>we</u> are going to do about the environment. As long as we are writing laws to make other people obey our notion of environmental care, there will be resistance. When enough of us as individuals start making good environmental choices there will be real change. That is the strength behind Durkheim's comment, "When people are moral, then no laws are necessary." Public education should be about creating that environmental consciousness where new laws are not necessary because people have internalized the idea of environmental care and made it part of their lives.

Right now we have **'environmentalism lite'; feels good, less, effective**. Public education is hard. Public education on caring for the environment is the work of generations and we are not doing it well, yet.

In the conclusion of their book, <u>Facts, Not Fear</u>, Sanera and Shaw write,

> "Environmental education should help students understand the complex living world and the natural laws or principles that govern it- that is it should be grounded in Science. In addition it should be taught with an understanding of economics, which is simply the study of why people make the choices they do" (Sanera and Shaw 233).

This appeal to good science is not casual rhetoric. As mentioned earlier, the point of Michael Crichton's novel <u>State of Fear</u> is that science gets lost in the shuffle when fear and politics are involved.

We do live in a complex world. Chaos theorists would remind us that the universe is not merely complex, but dynamically complex (Gleick 121). Fear distracts us from understanding. Sanera and Shaw are right, environmental education should be based on facts, not fear.

Reason Four:

Chicken Little and Addressing Risk

#4-I'll start believing the environmentalists when they stop acting like Chicken Little. I am now hearing reports that global temperatures will go up 20 degrees and the ocean levels will rise a meter in this century. Perhaps. But, they have been so wrong for so long I wonder how they have any credibility left. Malthus, two hundred years ago, and Paul Ehrlich, thirty years ago, said that population growth would outstrip our ability to feed ourselves. They were wrong. How can we believe these alarming claims when they have been so wrong for so long?

They have been so wrong, so often, how do they have any credibility left? In <u>Whole Earth Discipline</u> Stuart Brand carefully outlines how he and his environmental buddies were wrong about Population Growth and Nuclear Power. If they were so wrong on these issues, why should we believe them today on global climate change? Like Chicken Little they have damaged their own credibility.

Recovering Environmentalists

Perhaps Reality is the ultimate 12 Step Program. Whatever the reason, it is nice to see some prominent environmentalists changing their positions on some issues. Patrick Moore, one of the co-founders of Greenpeace dropped out of Greenpeace because he thought they had become "anti-science'(Moore). That some environmental groups ignored sound science was a conclusion many of us had come to years ago, but we were dismissed as merely being partisan. Bjorn Lomborg is a Danish professor of statistics. As a member of Greenpeace he was going to use his skills as a statistician to prove that the American business community was overstating their case when they said the global environmental conditions were not as bad as claimed by the environmental community (Lomorg xix). He ended up writing The Skeptical Environmentalist where he shows by statistical analysis that the business community was right after all, things are not as bad as the enviros had been saying. Lomborg was hammered by the environmental community for straying from the faith.

Gwyneth Cravens was one of the ring leaders against a proposed nuclear power plant on Long Island. She has since come to the conclusion that climate change is a bigger threat than any possible nuclear power disaster and wrote a book investigating the nuclear power industry titled, Power to Save the World: The Truth About Nuclear Energy.

Those of us who grew up during the 70's remember The Whole Earth Catalogue. Stewart Brand was the founding editor of The Whole Earth Catalogue and a life long environmental activist. In his 2009 book, "Whole Earth Discipline: An Ecopragmatist Manifesto", Brand lines out how he was wrong about population growth, nuclear power and genetically modified food.

There are two lessons I draw out from reading the accounts of how these passionate enviros changed their views. First, it's nice to know that the positions my neighbors and I have taken, and been criticized for, have been correct all along. Second, some of these people have been so wrong for so long I wonder why we even listen to them any more. This is important. I am not just taking a free throw here. There is a lot at stake on these issues. In our area, poor environmental policy cost 40,000 people their jobs one year (Howitt, et. al). The enviros shut down the timber industry in the Pacific Northwest to protect the spotted owl. Thousands of people lost their jobs and then we find out that spotted owl populations are falling inside Olympia National Park where logging is not an issue (NPR 5 August 2004). Ooops. Actually that's a pretty big "ooops."

Bad News Sells, But It May Not Make Good Policy

I understand, bad new sells. In the news business the old saying is, "If it bleeds, it leads." Bad news sells. Non-profit international aid societies went around for decades with hats in hand trying to raise money for Haiti. The 2010 earthquake hit and 'poof' the Red Cross raised tens of millions of dollars from people making donations- from their cell phones. It is the same way with environmental groups. It would be hard for them to raise money if everything was OK wouldn't it?

We have this problem in our own area. By the San Joaquin Air Pollution Control District's own measurements, air quality in our region is much better than twenty years ago. Specifically, particulate and nitrous oxide (NOX) emissions are down over sixty percent. You would think that would be a cause for celebration. Instead, the local daily paper and local environmental groups launch a crusade to clean up the Valley's air. Huh? They say we have the second or third dirtiest air basin in the nation. OK, but let's admit a couple of things. First, we have done a lot already. Second, they have moved the goal posts. Perhaps we do have the second or third dirtiest air in the nation. But, on what planet does a 60% improvement in air quality qualify as a 'sky is falling' disaster?

Why is this point so important? Because all the 'sky is falling' news gets in the way of good policy and real problem solving. Earlier, I mentioned the example of asthma and air quality- In our area the renewed concern about air quality was tied with studies showing increases in childhood asthma. In the minds of many, the two issues of air pollution and childhood asthma were linked. Ironically, at the same time the issue broke in our area a study was published in the British medical journal, The Lancet, showing childhood asthma was an *indoor* disease. Specifically, the study showed European farm kids had a lower incidence of asthma than their city cousins in spite of being exposed to more outside dust(Lancet). What was the difference between the two groups of kids? The farm kids spent more time outside and the city kids spent more time indoors, probably playing video games. I brought this study up to the environmental activists including an MD in respiratory therapy. They "knew" that childhood asthma was caused by dust from farms like mine and the solution was more regulations for farmers. Fortunately, we persisted. A few years later, the local branch of the American Lung Association started offering to help families do indoor assessments of their homes and cleanup of possible allergens. [It seems from their current website they have cancelled that program . But, they do have helpful tips online: http://www.lungusa.org/healthy-air/home/resources/keep-pollution-out-of-your-home.html]

There are a couple of lessons here. First, the 'sky is falling' mentality can lead to poor policy. To quote Larry Foulke, "We do not become safer by portraying the world unrealistically" (Cravens 309).

Second, we must remember the key to good policy is good information. Good science is based on objective data. In the social sciences, we are constantly reminded "Correlation does not equal causation." Just having a correlation is only the first step. You have to establish causation separately. In this case, there was no causal link between outdoor air quality and childhood asthma. In fact, they are negatively correlated. In our area the incidence of childhood asthma went up as air quality got better, not worse.

The Precautionary Principle

The driving force in assessing risk for many enviros is what is called the Precautionary Principle. "The Precautionary Principle says that if some course of action carries even a remote chance of irreparable damage to the ecology, then you shouldn't do it, no matter how great the possible advantages of that action may be" (Brand 158). That sounds pretty good doesn't it? The problem is it is a logical impossibility- you cannot prove a negative. I can say my fountain pen will not kill anyone. That is very probably true. But, there is probably some scenario where someone uses my pen to stab someone in the heart or it flies through the window in a train wreck, goes through a bystander's eye and kills them. Those are astronomically unlikely scenarios, but it shows I could never absolutely prove my pen will never kill anyone. You cannot prove a negative, and therein lies the problem with the Precautionary Principle. If we really believed in the Precautionary Principle, we probably wouldn't even get out of bed in the morning. But, we do have to get out of bed. Let's look at another example. An airplane designed along the lines of the Precautionary Principle will never get off the ground. In the spirit of the Precautionary Principle we demand absolute, 100%, forever guarantees, which are impossible. We can never design an airplane that is 100% guaranteed not to crash.

In his own critique of the Precautionary Principle, life-long environmental activist and <u>Whole Earth Catalogue</u> founder, Stewart Brand quotes

> "The Fable of the Steak Knives," as told by the founder of Wikipedia, Jimmy Wales. His software engineers were spending a lot of their time imagining problems that would occur in Wikipedia and then devising software solutions to head off the problems. He explained why that is the wrong approach:

> "You want to design a restaurant, and you think to yourself, "well, in this restaurant we're going to be serving steak, we're going to have steak knives, and since we are going to have steak knives, people might stab each other. How do we solve this problem? We're going to have to build cages around each table to make sure no one stabs each other.

> This makes for a bad society...when you try to prevent people from doing bad things, the very obvious side effect is that you prevent them from doing good things."

> The astronomical success of Wikipedia comes from its principle of not trying to solve imaginary problems but instead putting all of the community's efforts into close attention to what actually goes on, noting genuine problems as they emerge, and then solving them as locally as possible with speed and efficiency. The whole system is driven by success rather than problem driven (Brand 162).

I get it. Safety is crucial. No one is asking for permission to pollute. There are just better ways to manage risk than the Precautionary Principle.

This is another case of the fact that enviros have the luxury of not having to produce anything. It would be easy to invoke the Precautionary Principle on the farm if I didn't have to produce anything. In my case, I produce food and fiber to make a living and help meet the world's need to eat. At the 2001 World Economic Forum in Davos, Switzerland physicist-essayist Freeman Dyson said, "The European pretense of allowing no risk of irreparable damage makes no sense in the real world" (Brand 159). Brand follows with the reminder that, "Nothing is fully established scientifically, ever- not gravity, not Darwinian evolution, not the safety of peanut-better-&-jelly sandwiches. *Science is perpetual argument*" (Brand 161, italics mine).

Even the British House of Commons has realized there is a limit to the Precautionary Principle: "the House of Commons select committee on science and technology recommended that the term "should not be used and should 'cease to be included in policy guidance'" (Brand 163). I agree with Brand that we must always be vigilant on environmental issues, there is too much at stake. Politicians are not reliable watchdogs and there are people in the business community who put making a buck above doing the right thing. But, we must get beyond the log jam that is created by trying to enforce something like the Precautionary Principle. Fortunately, there is a solid, scientific alternative.

An Alternative to the Precautionary Principle

As noted earlier, Gwyneth Cravens is a life-long environmentalist who helped lead the fight against a nuclear power plant on Long Island in New York. She has since reconsidered her position on nuclear power. In her mind, the greater threat to the world today is carbon induced climate change and the best source of carbon free energy is nuclear power. She did not come to this position easily. In her book, Power to Save the World: The Truth About Nuclear Energy, Cravens writes of her investigation of the nuclear power industry from mining, at the beginning, to production to waste management at the end. She comes away with the confidence that nuclear power can be produced safely and that it is the only viable method of meeting our electricity baseload demands.

As a key part of her investigation, Cravens considered the idea of risk and nuclear power. Obviously, there is a lot at stake in this issue. A nuclear accident could be catastrophic and continued greenhouse gas production could also be catastrophic. As Dante was led on his tour by Virgil, Cravens was led on her investigation of the nuclear industry by Dr. D. Richard Anderson, a scientist with the Sandia National Lab in New Mexico. Anderson had a long career in nuclear power, program management and risk analysis. Anderson's method is different from the standard probability assessment that goes back to the time of Pascal. Dr. Anderson calls his method 'probabilistic risk assessment.'

"Probabilistic risk assessment, called in most other countries "probabilistic safety assessment," centered on the analysis of a hypothetical chain of mishaps as well as a distribution of scenarios generated by interacting events that could lead to a core meltdown and a radioactive release. This method is known as a fault-tree, or event tree, approach...In 1977, the NRC approved a peer review of the panel's finding that endorsed the PRA methodology as the best available tool" (Cravens 137).

Dr. Anderson notes that traditional methods of calculating risk are limited.

"The conservative estimates not only lead to uncertainty, but also lead to incorrect guidance from the analyses...That is, the calculations suggest that something will happen that cannot happen"(Cravens 138).

"Probability is a number expressing the likelihood that particular event will occur, expressed in a ratio of the actual number if occurrences to the number of possible occurrences. The traditional way of calculating such risks is deterministic...But if instead you choose the probabilistic approach, you take a sampling of the full range of each of the input variables so it gives a full range of output variables... and so it will tell you the probability of the occurrence of each of the answers you get. Probabilistic calculations are a huge number of deterministic ones summed up...when you do that you have the whole picture. You can see what's important and what's unimportant. If anybody comes in, say, from engineering, or geology, or microbiology and argues, 'You didn't include my value,' well, you could show that you had used it and that it did or did not have a great effect. Probabilistic risk assessment stopped all that terrible arguing that somebody or other had used the wrong value and therefore your calculation was invalid. PRA is more precise. It rules out the subjectivity in estimating the likelihood and consequences of events." (Cravens 138-9)

Anderson continues, with PRA-

"You can see objectively what's happening at every point on the curve...The outcomes in the extreme ends of the curve are so unlikely-having probability of occurrence of, say, less than 1 in 100 million – that you don't have to worry about them. PRA helps you guide the experiments you need to do, it eliminates the irrelevancies, the fluff, and at the end you've looked in detail at all the weaknesses and all the strengths and reduced the uncertainty, and you know where to spend time and funding most efficiently" (Cravens 140).

Anderson notes how fear and control of events are intertwined,

"People usually focus on consequence exclusively when they're in an unknown or new situation or one that's out of their control... when the event is unknown and scary... people automatically assume the probability of it occurring is high and so they get riveted on the consequence... That's called a worst case analysis. Troublemakers know we humans instinctively tend to do that, and they attempt to scare people into making bad decisions by always showing only worst-case consequences" (Cravens 140).

Letting fear drive the equation leads us to poor quality decisions.

"Conservative, rough estimates can therefore result in notions of extreme outcomes that may play to our worst fears and lead us to assume that consequences that are just about impossible in the real world are highly probable" (Cravens 140-1).

Not only can fear-based decisions led to poor quality decisions, but fear can be manipulated by people to further their particular cause, not merely the public good.

"I learned…that whenever you hear doomsday predictions made by trouble makers or con men who mislead people by using worst-case analysis, you should step back and ask what the probability- and therefore- the risk of the event is…don't just look at the consequences. If you can't make a reasonable estimate of the probability of an event, ask someone who's knowledgeable" (Cravens 142).

Dr. Anderson's conclusion is that Probabilistic Risk Assessment, PRA, is a better tool for assessing risk than traditional probability calculations. PRA can,

"be used to engage the community, to understand its responses, and to build people's particular interests and anxieties into an overall assessment of risks…Nothing is ever one hundred percent…[PRA] is a mathematically driven *philosophy*" (Cravens 143-144, italics hers).

Why Worst Case Scenarios Make for Poor Policy

Think about it, here's a worse case scenario of why Worse Case Scenarios don't work. Consider an airplane trip. What is the worst case scenario? The plane falls out of the sky. The only way to engineer an airplane that doesn't crash would make it so cumbersome it would never get off the ground. That wouldn't get us anywhere, would it?

Now, I understand the difference between a plane crash and a nuclear melt down. The worst case of an airplane crash is the tragedy of a few hundred people getting killed. That is bad, but it is a much smaller scale tragedy than the horrible nuclear meltdown scenarios dreamed up in Hollywood or by Greenpeace. But, let's get real- Hollywood is make believe and Greenpeace is trying to raise money. It is a lot easier to sell movies and raise money with the bogeyman of a possible nuclear disaster than it is to say, "Yep, they are right. The nuclear guys have created a safe system and it is getting better all the time."

There are better risk assessment tools than the Worst Case Scenario. We have looked at Probabilistic Risk Assessment, PRA. It is a sound scientific method that is not merely a good theory but a good practice.

Worst Case Scenarios sound good and they have their place in problem solving and disaster preparation. But, by using Worst Case Scenarios to shape our public policy, we paint ourselves into a corner we cannot get out of. Or, we tie ourselves in knots.There have been serious environmental concerns since at least the beginning of the Industrial Revolution. Starting with Malthus at the beginning of the Industrial Revolution, people have been running around like Chicken Little saying, "The sky is falling." I don't mean to mock our environmental friends and neighbors, but they have been so wrong for so long, I wonder why we even listen. Of course, one of the reasons we listen is fear. Bad news sells newspapers, books and air time. But, does bad news get us anywhere? If you remember the story of Chicken Little, she got her friends all wound up and running around too. That didn't work out so well for them. They got eaten by the fox. Just as fear drove Chicken Little and her friends to doing fatally foolish, things we are at risk of letting our fears drive us to do foolish things. It is time we took a more reasonable look at our fears and how to address risk in what we do.

Reason Three:

Seeing the Big Picture

#3-I'll believe the Environmentalists when they have a view of the Big Picture. They teach us that life is an inter-connected web and then they focus on their special interest. I have sat in too many meetings where specialists have dug in their heels, not willing to compromise or even discuss any other issues until their concern was fully settled. Environmental problems are, by nature, system-wide problems. They need big picture solutions. For example, hybrid cars will save gas. What are we planning to do with all those used hybrid batteries?

In 1994 I served as the token farmer on a technical advisory committee of Central California Regional Water Quality Control Board. The issue we were dealing with was non-point source pollution. Point source pollution is the stuff coming out of factory discharge pipes. It had taken over twenty years to clean up point source pollution, and that was the easy stuff. Non-point source pollution is harder. How do you decide where the pollutants are coming from and how do you stop it when there is no focused point of pollution? One example is the brake lining dust and oils that drip off our cars and trucks onto the road ways. When it rains, this stuff washes into our lakes and rivers. Dealing with those kinds of contaminants is qualitatively more difficult than cleaning up a factory discharge pipe. And remember, it took over twenty years to deal with easy stuff like factory discharge pipes.

OK, back to the technical advisory committee I served on, once upon a time. That was an interesting experience. The issue we were dealing with was non-point source pollution from farms. For example, how do we deal with fertilizer and pesticide runoff from farm fields? A good question. Remember, I was the token farmer. The other people in the room were engineers and regulators each responsible for dealing with the various problems. One guy was responsible for salts. The next guy was an expert on fertilizer. The next guy's specialty was pesticides. The real problem was that these guys were locked into their area of expertise. Each one was convinced their area was the most important and they were not willing to sign off on anything until their concern was taken care of. The salt guy wanted all the salt problems from every farm taken care of before he was willing to consider anyone else's issue. The pesticide guy was the same way. So was the fertilizer guy. We were in gridlock for months.

In her book, <u>The Watchman's Rattle</u>, Rebecca Costa calls this 'silo thinking.' Costa defines silo thinking as, "compartmentalized thinking and behaviors that prohibit the coloration needed to address highly complex problems" (Costa 131). Silo thinking, according to Costa is one of the handful of mental barriers that prohibit us from solving the problems facing humanity today. Her concern is that if we don't overcome these barriers our species is at risk. I don't know if our species is at risk. Remember, I am not convinced the sky is falling. What I do know is that silo thinking makes problem solving much more difficult.

I am a generalist living in a world of specialists. I have learned to appreciate our specialists. Because of the skills of specialist we have the technical wonders of our day. I am a big fan of their work. I probably wouldn't be here if it weren't for the work of specialists in modern medicine. The problem with specialists is that while they are great in their area of expertise, they are severely limited in other areas. What's the old saying about knowing more and more about less and less?

Costa writes,

Silos exist everywhere. The CIA doesn't speak to the FBI and the physics department doesn't set foot in the economics building. Environmentalists don't talk to oil executives, defendants don't talk to prosecutors, Republicans don't talk to Democrats, doctors don't talk to insurance companies, and Al-Qaeda doesn't talk to anyone.

And we wonder why society is gridlocked and broad, complex, systemic problems continue to worsen (Costa 132).

Costa quotes Dean Kamen, the inventor of the Segway scooter, as believing,

> "the biggest challenge the U.S. faces isn't technology, but rather silo thinking...[because] silo thinking makes it extremely difficult to fix a systemic problem because no one silo is responsible for the overall problem" (Costa 136).

That is the problem I found on the technical advisory committee. We were gridlocked in the face of a broad, systemic problem because each of our experts was hunkered down in his silo. E. O. Wilson describes what he calls "professional atomization" (Wilson 144). That is another good description, especially if we use the original, ancient Greek notion of atoms. We were encapsulated and sealed off from one another. Costa quotes writer Saul Kaplan,

> It is not the technology that that gets in the way of innovation. It is the human beings and organizations we live in that are both stubbornly resistant to experimentation and change. If we want to make progress in the big issues of our time, we have to look up from our silos and become more comfortable recombining capabilities in new ways in order to connect with the unusual suspects (Costa 145).

Whether it is atomization or silos the answer is the same, we need to look at the bigger picture if we are going to solve the large, complex problems of our day.

So, what did we do on the technical advisory committee? We found a solution.

Actually, as the generalist in a roomful of specialists I found a solution when I reached back to my junior high science class with Miss Dunkl. Do you remember the Scientific Method? I suggested we create a version of the Scientific Method where we could take each of the issues the committee was assigned and use that framework to deal with the problem. It was a simple, elegant solution. My colleagues were so happy with the solution, they suggested that I make the presentation to the regional water board and the EPA when we made our final report. [I am pretty sure that was a compliment and not punishment. Either way, it was the price of opening my big bazoo.]

Exporting Jobs and the Big Picture

Another example of seeing the big picture is the discussion of exporting jobs. Yes, some companies move their factories overseas because of cheaper labor. Is it at least possible that regulatory costs are an issue?

As a farmer, in today's globalized market, I have to compete with every farmer on the planet who thinks he can grow cotton or wheat. All of my costs are higher than my competitors. My labor costs are already higher by orders of magnitude. I don't begrudge my employees their wages. They work hard and they work smart. I would love to pay them more. All I am saying is that we are competing with countries that pay their workers two and three dollars a day. Now add regulatory costs. This is no joke. American Farm Bureau President Bob Stallman reported, ten years ago, that regulations costs American farmers $20 billion dollars a year. No matter how you slice it, that is a lot of money. [The real irony is that, at the time, people were arguing that the costs of farm price support programs were too expensive. Do you want to guess what the estimated farm price support programs cost? You guessed it- $20 billion per year. My response as a farmer? It's a wash. Stop complaining about the price supports, they are paying for the regulatory costs that are imposed on farmers. Of course, with the 2012 Farm Bill, they are cutting price supports and leaving the regulations in place for the farmers to absorb.]

Back to my main point here, I think regulatory costs are just as much of a reason why businesses move production off shore as their desire for cheap labor. In terms of seeing the big picture, can you see what happens when we don't look at the bigger picture? Activists and critics tend to reduce complex problems to simplistic solutions. I get it. As an essayist, I write in an effort to make complex problems easier to understand. But, what I am talking about is qualitatively different. Understandable doesn't mean simplistic. The world is complex. Costa wonders if, "sometimes the big picture is just too big" (Costa 131). Mystics and Chaos theorists would agree with Costa that some things are beyond human understanding. Offering simplistic, one dimensional solutions to the problems that face our world does not help us create workable solutions. In fact, simplistic answers can make things more difficult because they ignore important realities. For example, let's take my example about exporting jobs. If we just say manufacturers are looking for cheap labor and we ignore the rising cost of regulation, what happens? Manufacturers will export more jobs because the cost of production keeps getting higher.

Do you want to know what the real irony is? Not only are jobs lost, but the concerns that prompt regulations are not addressed either. Labor activists want safer, higher paying jobs for workers. That is a good goal. Do workers get safer and higher paying jobs when manufacturers go overseas? No. Advocates want stricter environmental regulations. When manufacturing is driven overseas by higher regulatory costs, does the environment get better protection? No. So, ironically, by offering simplistic solutions, environmental activists may clean up one site here at home, but they cost people their jobs and export the pollution somewhere else.

What we need are well-rounded solutions. One of my accusations is the environmental community is not interested in problem solving. They are not willing to roll up their sleeves and do the real hard work of finding technical solutions to real hard technical problems. It is easier to file lawsuits and lobby for regulations. Those are arrogant, top down methods. You don't like pesticides? Great, neither do I. Help me find a way to protect my crops and produce food without them. You don't like air pollution? Great, neither do I. Help me find a way to run my tractors with cleaner engines. Don't just lobby the government to raise standards. You are concerned about how we use natural resources? Great, so am I. Help us find ways to use natural resources and care for the environment. But, please don't sit in your silo and refuse to work on anyone else's issues until all of your concerns are addressed. I can assure you that while your concerns may be valid, they are only one part of a very complex picture.

I teach critical thinking and problem solving. One of the things I encourage my students to do is see the big picture. One exercise we do is a full contact debate. Each learning team is required to prepare both sides of a debate question. They literally do not find out which side of the debate they are going to have to present until I flip a coin as they go up and start the debate. For the record, they usually hate that. It is easy to prepare for and debate passionately about something you believe in. The hard part of this assignment is learning about the other side's position well enough that you can understand and argue their side of the issue.

John Wesley Powell led the first white water expeditions through the Grand Canyon. Powell was one of those amazing 19th Century all-around guys. He was a soldier who lost an arm at the Battle of Shiloh during the Civil War. He was a scientist, explorer, and a social reformer. His knowledge was encyclopedic. A driving principle of Powell's was caught in the title of an anthology of his writings; Powell was committed to "seeing things whole." Seeing things whole is what is lacking in a world of specialists and what is desperately needed in an increasingly complex world.

John Muir is often quoted as saying, "When we try to pick out anything by itself, we find it hitched to everything else in the universe" (Muir 211). This quote is usually mentioned by those who want to remind us that the natural world is an integrated whole, and that is a great reminder. I would remind us this quote also tells us that the economy and the environment are tied together. We too are a part of the natural world. I will readily admit that we have to understand that our economy is set within the environment. Can you also admit that the environment is tied to the economy? Do you doubt me on this question? Look at Al Gore's book, Earth in the Balance. His opening example of environmental disaster comes from the former Soviet Union; where they drained the Aral Sea for irrigation (Gore 19ff). We haven't done anything like that in a capitalist economy have we? For an air quality disaster Gore doesn't highlight New York or LA, but Romania under Soviet rule (Gore 81ff). Bailey makes similar observations about East Germany after Soviet occupation. When East Germany opened and the process of reunifying Germany began they found huge issues in air, water and soil pollution (Bailey 488.) Apparently the "workers' paradise" was not only an economic disaster, but an ecological disaster as well.

Our goal should be balance- a healthy environment and a healthy economy go hand in hand.

Reason Two:

Environmental Hypocrites?

#2-I will start believing the environmentalists when they start living themselves the life style they recommend for the rest of us. I really respect the advocates who actually ride their bicycles. But, don't live a modern lifestyle and then complain about everyone else living one.

OK, I know the term "Environmental Hypocrites" will offend some people. Of course in our politically correct age I am not sure I can say anything without the risk of offending someone. That's why I put in a question mark; I am raising a question.

There are actually two things I would like to address here. One is the question of hypocrisy. The other question is- Is environmentalism a religion? We'll get to hypocrisy in a moment. The idea that the environmental movement is a religion is not as far fetched as it may sound, at first.

I teach world religions at the college level. One of the exercises I walk through with my students is a matrix I have created to compare and contrast different religions. We consider things like sacred writings, sacred times, and sacred places. We also consider the rules by which people are expected to live under. Looking at it from that angle doesn't environmentalism look like a religion?

Sacred writings? How about Thoreau, Muir and Rachel Carson?

Sacred times? How about Earth Day, or summer solstice?

Sacred places? How about Yosemite, or Mt Shasta? The Himalayas, lakes, rivers or beaches?

Rules? How about reduce, recycle and re-use?

I'll go after the rule one a little later. Another irony I see, is that if you ask the generation that drives the environmental movement about morality, in most things they will tell you they don't believe in an ethical 'black and white'. They see large gray areas. But, when it comes to their issues, they sure think things are 'black and white' don't they?

Consider the car you drive; large cars are not environmentally correct are they? How about the home you live in; do you know how the enviros want us to live? Packed in high-density cities to minimize our footprint. I get it. We can't have mass transit until we pack enough people together. But, on other issues these people are advocates of choice. Where is the choice in this? Does everyone really want to live in chic lofts downtown- all their lives? Have they considered the psychological and social consequences of people packed together like that? Living in Tribeca, Greenwich or DuPont Circle might be cool when you are single and twenty-something. Do you really want to raise kids there? I wouldn't. I know we can't all live out in rural areas, but I really like what Walt Whitman said,

"Now I see the secret of making the best persons,
It is to grow in the open air and eat and sleep with the earth."
(Whitman 125).

There is another irony, the same people who want us to learn to love and respect nature want to isolate us from nature. How can we "grow in the open air and eat and sleep with the earth" if we are crammed in cities. Please don't tell me urban parks. I love visiting the great city parks when I travel, but neither Central Park in New York, Golden Gate Park in San Francisco nor Hyde Park in London are natural.

Returning to my question- Is environmentalism a religion? I will leave it for you to answer for yourself. I think environmentalism does bear the marks of a religion, sacred writings, sacred times and sacred places. I think the enviros have a very strong ethic by which they would like all of us to live. I consider today's enviros to be the new Puritans, or maybe the New Inquisition.

Actually, I like the old Puritans. We make fun of them, but I respect the sincerity of the pursuit of their faith. How do we caricature them? Self-righteous? Legalistic? Busy bodies telling everyone how to live their lives? Can you see where I am going with this? Without ever admitting it, today's enviros have become the new Puritans. Have you ever come across someone who is More-Environmental-Than-Thou? You know what I am talking about don't you? How about legalistic? If you don't buy fair-trade this, or do that, you are not doing it right are you? How about right belief? Do you know the name for those who don't believe in global warming? Global warming deniers? Really? Are you going to label me the same way we label those who don't believe in historic fact of the Holocaust just because I don't find your science convincing? Wow! What happened to free thought?

The real irony is that same people who promote environmentalism with religious fervor bristle when people of other religions try to live out their faiths. So much for tolerance.

Are Enviros Hypocritical?

Now, to the real question of hypocrisy. I find it utterly ironic that I have come across so many enviros who criticize my use of resources as a farmer yet they are strapped with all the conveniences of modern life. I am not just talking about their smart phones, laptop computers and hybrid cars. I go up in the Sierras and they are not wearing wool or using down sleeping bags, they are wearing synthetic fleece and using poly fill bags. Whatever you want to say about them, the fleece and poly fill are not natural. I understand the performance characteristics of modern fibers. I just want to remind you how un-natural they are and what it takes to produce them.

Elsewhere, I have mentioned Gandhi's honesty. As a pacifist, he helped form an ambulance corps for the British during the Boer War in South Africa (Gandhi 214ff). He understood that even though he did not carry a gun he was part of the war effort. There is honesty and integrity in that position. The enviros I come across today don't seem to have that honesty and integrity. They have split the world into Us and Them. "Us" are the ones who care for the natural world. Whatever "We" do is OK. "They" are the ones who don't care for the natural world. Whatever "They" do is wrong. I don't think this distinction is fair. The issue is caring for the environment. Driving a hybrid car still adds greenhouse gases to the atmosphere. They may add less greenhouse gases, but they are still adding greenhouse gases to the atmosphere. The greenhouse gases don't automatically disappear because you like the environment.

The real problem with this mental hypocrisy is that it interferes with real problem solving. As long as it is "Us" versus "Them" we are not work together on solving problems. We are spending our time face to face arguing, instead of side by side working on solutions.

One of the most pernicious examples is the notion of the Zero Sum game. I was meeting with a prominent Bay Area environmentalist on water issues. As I asked questions about various solutions to the problems facing the San Francisco Bay- Sacramento Delta. After shooting down each solution I offered he looked at me and said, "You don't understand. It is a Zero Sum game." What he was saying was we cannot work together on problem solving.

I teach critical thinking and problem solving. One of the principles of interest based negotiations is, "Invent options for mutual gain" (Fisher and Ury 56ff). When you are looking at things as a Zero Sum Game you are not working to "invent options for mutual gain," you are trying to grab all the marbles you can. When it comes to every environmental issue I can think of, that is how the enviros are acting. They are grabbing all the marbles they can. Once again the "Us/Them" attitude prevents problem solving.

Some of this may be rooted in the idea I have mentioned above. For many in the environmental movement this is religion and a common practice in religion is to take the high moral ground and accept no compromise. Things makes sense when you understand environmentalism as a religion. Anything less than the pure faith is compromise. Religious people are notorious for their resistance to compromise. I respect people who live out their values so, in one sense, I have no problem with resistance to compromise. In fact, I personally don't like compromise. Built into the notion of compromise is that we each give up something to reach agreement. We give up half a loaf to keep half a loaf. I think we all naturally resist giving up something, especially when we believe we are morally right. I think the wiser option is "Invent Options for Mutual Gain," the proverbial "Win/Win." You don't even bother seeking mutual benefit when you think things are a Zero-Sum game. Seeking mutual benefit is hard to do, but in the long run I think it is the most constructive. When everyone benefits you don't have anyone trying to previous agreements.

OK, accusing people of hypocrisy is pretty harsh. I don't mean to be mean, but what else can I call it? We have people who stake out the high moral ground and preach at the rest of us and yet their personal choices do not reflect their own ethics, which they preach to us. Is that not the very definition of hypocrisy?

The ancient Greek philosophers believed that public speakers needed three things to be effective: logos, pathos, and ethos. "Logos" is a word, something worth saying. "Pathos" is an emotional, sympathetic connection with the listener. "Ethos", the word we got our word 'ethics' from, refers to our habits. When the CEO of Starbucks spends forty years talking about how ethical a company they are and after forty years less than fifty percent of their coffee is ethically sourced- he has undercut his own ethos, his own ethical credibility (Shultz 204). When he talks about how environmentally sound Starbucks is and they don't even have a plan to recycle a single coffee cup for the first forty years of Starbuck's existence, they have undercut their own ethos, their own ethical credibility (Shultz 324).

I don't mean to bash Starbucks. They are merely a handy example. There are many others like them. I have mentioned before about the times I have been at meetings where environmental activists come to testify for their cause and they arrive in fossil fuel burning cars, toting their cell phones and laptops. Their lifestyle is indistinguishable from the people they are protesting. 'Poof', there goes some of their credibility.

I really respect the people who grow their own organic vegetables and ride their bikes to work. My daughter traded in her Dodge Durango and bought a little Hyundai. Another friend traded in his full-size SUV and bought a Prius. This is what we need, people making personal choices that make a difference for the environment.

Reason One:

The Enviros Have Already Won!

#1- I'll believe the environmentalists when they realize they have already won.

The air is cleaner and our rivers don't catch fire like they once did. There is tremendous public support for the environment. The tide is in their favor. They should celebrate their victory and lead us onward and upward instead of beating us over the head and dragging us from one crisis to the next.

The enviros have won- and yet they still act like the sky is falling.

The enviros have won- they have convinced us that we should care for the environment. Environmental policy drives state and federal legislation. Environmental policy drives corporations in products and procedures. Recently (March 2011) I was talking with a professor who has worked for both the University of California and the California State University system. He said that concerns over global climate change are driving research in every department. I am confident that we could poll any room full of people in America and they would, by and large, consider themselves environmentalists. A recent student of mine did her persuasive speech on going green. She couldn't think of any criticisms to address in her presentation because, as she said, "everyone is for the environment." The enviros have won.

You don't have to convince me that we should care for the environment. I grew up in the 70's as this all came to a boil. My personal theology is that we have been deputized by the Creator as caretakers of the planet. [Of course, our record isn't that impressive. I would attribute that to the fact that we forgot our calling for a long time.]

You don't have to convince me. I want to care for the natural world- show me how! What I don't see from the environmental community is helpful 'how to's". How can I farm in a more environmental sound manner and still be productive? The environmental community is not helpful with technical answers. I have to go to the universities or industry for answers.

What I do see from the enviros are lawsuits and legislation. To be honest, this rarely helps. What I don't need is another regulation telling me to lower my greenhouse gas emissions. What I need is research that shows us methods to lower our greenhouse gas emissions. What I don't need is another regulation that says lower my fossil fuel consumption. What I need is research that shows how I can use conservation tillage in my soil and cover crops to lower my need for synthetic fertilizers. What I don't need is someone telling me to grow organic cotton. What I need is someone to show me how to kill plant bugs and defoliate my cotton with greener methods. These are serious concerns and difficult technical problems. They aren't solved with wishful thinking. The batteries on my magic wand wore out years ago. These are difficult problems and I could use some help from the environmental community in solving them, instead of harassment.

I asked a self-proclaimed radical environmentalist, (the grad school professor I have mentioned earlier), "Why do we see only lawsuits from the environmental community instead of real help solving problems?" His response was enlightening: "Business people are innovative. They'll figure it out." Wow. That seems a little arrogant to me. They stake out the high moral ground. From that lofty position, they tell us what to do. They won't get in the trenches and help us figure out the solutions. On top of that, my experience is that when we on the ground do figure out how to address their concerns- they move the goal posts. We have had the experience, here, in Central California. Air quality is significantly better than it was twenty years ago. Particulate and nitrous oxide emissions are down over 60% by the air districts own measurements and the enviros say we are still in violation of federal air standards. Perhaps, but that is mainly because they tightened the standards, they moved the goal posts. I am all in favor of clean air, I am all in favor of even cleaner air, but their method of lawsuit and regulation hasn't solved the problem. What has solved the problem was nuts and bolts research to help solve difficult technical problems.

Do you want to know what a farmer thinks about the endless waves of environmental rules and regulations? I make my living producing food and fiber, not going to meetings and filling out forms. My margins are so thin that one hail storm or one bug invasion can wipe me out for the year. I have neither the time nor the money to jump through hoops. If you have an innovation or a practice that works, I'm your man. But, come along side me and show me how it works, don't mandate it from on high. Farmers have seen enough snake oil salesmen. One guy had a fuel conditioner that was supposed to lower fuel consumption and increase power on our tractors. He couldn't explain how it worked. Another guy had a fifty thousand dollar apparatus that you could splice into your water well discharge pipe and it would take all the salts out of the water. He could not tell us how his magic pipe worked, that was a trade secret. I have seen an endless procession of foliar sprays that would solve all my plant problems from bugs to the heartbreak of psoriasis.

As I have said before, no one is asking permission to rape and pillage the environment. I am a simple guy, show me how to grow food and care for the planet and I am in.

I have had environmentalists come and wave their magic wands and say, "Do this and all your problems will go away." It doesn't work that way. Weeds and bugs don't kill themselves. I don't buy herbicides because I am married to the chemical companies. I buy herbicides to kill weeds that steal water and nutrients from my crops. Yes, with better management, I can use less herbicides. But, the batteries on my magic wand wore out years ago. There is no magic involved. It takes solid research and realistic management to solve these problems. Let's look at drip irrigation as an example. We have known about drip irrigation for decades. But, it has only been the last few years when farmers and irrigation companies have learned to apply drip irrigation on a commercial scale. It is a system-sized solution that requires changes in tillage equipment as well as installation of new irrigation equipment. The results have been impressive.

Innovation takes smart work, not wishful thinking. Let's look at drip irrigation. Let's look at solar power. Let's look at cleaner burning diesel engines. What I am asking for is help to solve these problems. The enviros have won, we agree that we shouldn't pollute the environment. Now show us how.

Summary: Finding Balance

My favorite Clint Eastwood movie is "Heartbreak Ridge". Clint's character, Gunnery Sergeant Tim Highway, teaches a Recon unit to "Adapt, innovate and overcome." That is the kind of can-do attitude that is missing in our environmental debates.

What are the principles of Safe and Sane Environmental Policy?

I have had my opportunity to state my case of where I think the environmental movement has been unreasonable. I don't want to stand accused of the same offense of not offering solutions. Below, I will line out some basic principles that can guide us past the grid-lock that we face on environmental issues.

Balance

The first principle in a safe and sane environmental policy is balance. We can neither let unrestrained pollution take place, nor can we let the Precautionary Principle strangle progress. The principle that must guide us is a healthy environment <u>and</u> a healthy economy.

As I say in Reason #1, There is tremendous public support for the environment. The reason I specifically say a "healthy environment" is that a healthy environment is different than trying to turn back the clock. The fact is that we cannot have 35 million people in California, 300 million people in the United States and 7 billion people worldwide without having some environmental impact. Yes, I know people have been concerned about the global population since the time of Malthus. I would even agree that fewer people on the planet would be good for the environment. The problem is that I don't see anyone offering to check out. We have to live with the current population numbers. There are even projections the global population might grow to 10 billion, or more (Avery 48ff). That actually makes the argument for finding a healthy balance between the environment and the economy even more urgent. We cannot ignore the problem and we cannot allow gridlock to continue.

A healthy environment may not be a totally natural environment. You cannot put 35 million people in California, 300 million in the US, and 7 billion on the planet without some environmental impact. But, a healthy environment will have clean water, clean air *and* a reasonable use of natural resources.

This is what the rub on environmental issues comes down to– *what is the reasonable use of our natural resources?* Industrialists in the past have said, "We can have it all" and ignored the consequences. We have seen practices like clear cutting of forests and hydraulic mining in California a century ago. The pendulum has swung back in the other direction in the recent years to the point where those wishing to produce needed goods for our society are handcuffed by environmental restrictions. [Remember, I find it highly ironic that many who criticize manufacturers for taking the factories over seas all support the regulations that make manufacturing here in the US prohibitive. There is a connection.]

One of my professors at in grad school is a self-proclaimed "radical environmentalist". I asked him what he thought was the appropriate use of natural resources. His answer was, "no one has the answer to this question" (personal correspondence). I agree that no one has the mathematical answer to this question. But, I think we can answer the question in principle. We should be allowed to utilize natural resources, but not to the point of depletion. Theodore Roosevelt and Gifford Pinchot pioneered this idea a century ago. Pinchot pioneered sustainable timber harvests.

I also agree that an ultimate solution to our environmental issues will require at least a rethinking of the issues by all, and making major changes in how we live our lives as individuals and as communities

I think there is more to a healthy environment and healthy economy than "Reduce, Re-use, Recycle." That is a start, but it doesn't address the underlying premise of our consumer society. When I say a healthy economy, I think we must address the unquestioned materialism of a consumer culture. Addressing materialism and our consumer society is far too large a subject to address here, but I would like to make a couple of points.

I still find it ironic that the environmental movement and the Christian community tend to view each other with some level of suspicion. There are some historical reasons for this mutual suspicion that go back to the founding of the environmental movement. The irony is this, both the historic church and the environmental movement share a concern about materialism. The medieval church criticized the materialism of the Renaissance and Enlightenment because it threatened their power. But, their real criticism was that materialism focused merely on our physical life and they taught the importance of spiritual matters. The modern environmental movement is also concerned that there is more to life than the things offered by our consumer culture. Both the historic church and the modern environmental movement agree that modern consumerism neglects something important. It is sad and ironic that they have not been able to effectively join forces and address a mutual concern. Ultimately, both agree that the notion, "He who dies with the most toys wins" is a silly notion that highlights that there is more to life than the things we own. I am writing this chapter during Christmas vacation. One big stress during Christmas is, 'what to buy the person who has everything." That notion alone should give us pause. The holidays themselves remind us that after the packages are opened and the gifts perhaps forgotten, that faith and family are at the core of the season and at the core of our lives.

No Turning Back

What it comes down to is we basically like the benefits of modern life. I, for one, like having my food cooked and sleeping indoors at night. We also like the benefit of modern medicine and the extended life spans we enjoy. We tend to take many of these things for granted. For example, we forget that the average life span in the US a century ago was in the mid-40's, today it is in the mid-80's. That didn't happen by accident. Extended life spans are a direct benefit of modern life. Now what we must do is discover how to maintain the benefits of modern life, indeed to continue progress, while caring for the environment.

In his book "No Turning Back," former environmental lobbyist Wallace Kaufmann notes,

"There is no turning back. We can find beauty, knowledge and insight in the cultures of the Bushmen and Buddhists, but so far only Western science and technology continue to provide for the material needs of the world's people. A movement that rejects this tradition is dangerously out of touch with reality, and cavalierly robs less fortunate people of their best hope" (Kaufmann 14).

Farmers and the Social Contract

I teach business ethics at the college level. One of the issues we talk about in class is the Social Contract. The idea of a social contract goes back at least as far as Kant and Rousseau. The basic questions in the Social Contract are-

"What is the responsibility of society to the individual?"

And

"What is the responsibility of the individual to society?"

Two great questions and you can imagine the class discussions we have.
More specific questions would be-

"What is the responsibility of farmers to society?"

And

"What is society's responsibility to our farmers?"

We do not normally think of things this way. As a farmer I accept that farmers have a responsibility to grow safe food. The good news is we do that well. Society adds other responsibilities and we comply. Agrarian Wendell Berry suggests that, therefore society should support farmers. And, here is where this particular social contract breaks down.

We live in an open economy, meaning we import and export at will. The social contract with farmers breaks down when farmers accept the higher costs of society's demands, in the form of regulations, and then consumers buy their food from somewhere else because it is cheaper.

Please trust me, I understand the importance of a bargain. But, can you see how insisting one side hold up their end of the social contract and the other side free to break the social contract is fundamentally unfair?

If we are serious about maintaining a social contract-

If we are serious about clean air and clean water-

Then we need farmers to support the farmers who grow their food and maintain their end of the social contract and not buy imported food just because it is cheaper.

The Problem with the Environmentalist Position

The enviros demand absolute certainty in the name of the Precautionary Principle. It is a logical impossibility. The enviros have no responsibility to produce anything. If, by use of the Precautionary Principle, nothing gets done they are OK with that. They have met their goal of not impacting the environment. But those of us who, for example, want to eat are left in the lurch, because those of us who produce food have had our hands tied by the enviros.

The enviros have no responsibility to produce food, clothing, housing, or transportation. Agreed, there are some assumptions built into that statement. What are legitimate necessities? We may not need a summer cabin in the mountains or a boat and an RV, but that is not what I am talking about. What I am talking about is more basic- food, shelter and healthcare for all. If the enviros want to have a discussion about American consumerist lifestyles, that is a great and important discussion. But, have you noticed how rarely they bring that up? They probably know if they mess with our lifestyles, they will lose support. Again, as Kaufmann has written, we are not turning back.

My point on the issue of responsibility is rooted in my experience as a farmer. The enviros who want to cut off my water supply don't care if we produce food or fiber. Their cause is protecting the environment. They usually assume that all farmers are rich, fat cats. But, that is a red herring. The heart of the issue is, as I have tried to lay out in Reason 10, is about the use of our natural resources. The enviros have zero responsibility to produce anything. So, logically, their position is that we cannot use any natural resources because that would affect the environment which is their prime concern. Their Prime Directive is to do no harm to the environment. The problem with their position is twofold. First, every other species modifies its environment. I don't see beavers taking out permits to build their dams. Second, it allows us virtually no reasonable method to take care of our needs for food and shelter.

I think, in the end, this is why support for the environmental movement is limited. People want to do the right thing and feel good about doing the right thing. But, in the end they know, deep down an absolute environmental position is unreasonable.

This is another reason why I think we must find balance on environmental issues. This will be hard. The enviros have religious zeal and do not easily consider compromise. Their cause is a moral cause, a moral crusade and moral crusaders consider compromise of their values to be heresy. They have no responsibility to produce anything so they can draw the line at the point of absolute protection of the environment. Only those of us who have been in some form of production industry can understand the day-to-day difficulty of balancing income, expenses and productivity.

Let's say, for example, we let the enviros win in their absolutist cause. Where will you get your food and clothing? The groceries you bought this week didn't arrive through warm thoughts and good intentions. The food we eat is produced by the hard work of a long line of people before it makes it to your plate. If we count on the enviros and their methods, people will starve.

Again, I advocate balance- of course we care for the environment, but we also utilize natural resources to produce the things we need. This is what I mean by a healthy environment *and* a healthy economy.

Some of us consider care of the environment a mandate our species was given by the Creator at the dawn of time. Some of us consider care of the environment to be our responsibility because we are the most highly developed members of the animal kingdom. Either way, I accept our responsibility to care for the environment. But, I accept that responsibility with one proviso. I want the ability to utilize natural resources. There in lies the problem. Ethics is easy in one dimension. We all agree that taking a life is wrong. We also agree in women's rights. But, when we put those two together, we end up with one of the most controversial issues in our society. We have a similar problem here- we agree we should care for the environment <u>and</u> we must use natural resources to produce food, clothing and shelter.

Lomborg makes an interesting comment on the balance between the economy and the environment at the beginning and the end of his book, <u>The Skeptical Environmentalist</u>:

> In general we need to confront our myth of the economy undercutting the environment. We have grown to believe that we are faced with an inescapable choice between higher economic welfare and a greener environment. But surprisingly and as will be documented in [his] book, environmental development often stems from economic development-only when we get sufficiently rich can we afford the relative luxury of caring for the environment…higher income in general is correlated with higher environmental sustainability (32-33).

In addition to balancing a healthy environment and a healthy economy may I suggest we look back at the work of Albert Schweitzer as an alternative to the gridlock we face on environmental issues?

Schweitzer Revisited: An Environmental Ethic for the 21st Century

Our Place in Nature

The place of humanity in the natural order has been a question since the beginning. Various faiths and philosophies have sought to describe our place. It is a fundamental question and should be asked and answered in every generation.

For most of history mere survival has been the issue. Nature was an opponent. Forests were dark and wilderness was dangerous. Civilization was seen as the answer Now, there are so many of us and our civilization has had such an impact on the world that some question not only our survival but also the survival of the natural world. They question our right to affect other species or use resources.

Reverence for Life

A century ago, a remarkable man raised as an ethic the Reverence for Life. Albert Schweitzer's thoughts were seen as too lofty and idealistic and were hence ignored. What Schweitzer offers us, today, is the basis for a non-sectarian ethic as we face the challenges of the Twenty First Century.

"I am life which wills to live in the midst of life which wills to live."

Albert Schweitzer (Philosophy 309)

This is the starting point for Schweitzer. He goes on further to add to the problem. [We are] "...subject to the puzzling and horrible law of being obliged to live at the cost of other life, and to incur again and again the guilt of destroying life"(Schweitzer Life 188). I think that legitimate guilt is what encourages some people to become vegetarians. The Jains in India go even further. They are known for, among other things, wearing masks to prevent them from accidentally inhaling small bugs.

For Schweitzer, the next step is thought. [For the person] "... who has become a thinking being feels a compulsion to give to every will-to-live the same reverence for life that he gives to his own"(Schweitzer Life 186).

Life is Sacred

A reverence for life is rooted in the understanding that life is sacred. The notion that life is sacred neither presumes nor precludes God in the Judeo-Christian sense. The nature of God is an issue to be dealt with elsewhere.That life is sacred is the only possible position in establishing an environmental ethic. Without the principle that life is sacred you are left with legitimized savagery- mere survival of the fittest. As Schweitzer notes- "Nature knows no similar reverence for life"(Schweitzer Reverence 120).

What is established is that humanity is somehow different than the rest of the natural order. Either humanity is different from the rest of the natural world and hence a moral responsibility can be imposed on us –or– We are no different than the rest of the natural world and we have no more moral responsibility than a coyote has to a jackrabbit.

Aldo Leopold writes, "An ethic, ecologically speaking is a limitation on freedom of action in the struggle for existence" (Leopold 238). Schweitzer would agree. "A man is really ethical only when he obeys the constraint laid upon him to help all life able to succor and when he goes out of his way to avoid injuring anything living"(Schweitzer 310). But the question stands-What other species limits its freedom in the struggle for existence? Even weeds grow to fill the empty spaces, pushing through pavement in the struggle for existence.

There is a desire by the environmental movement to impose morality on humanity with regards to the environment. That is fine. But, you cannot impose morality without some sense that life is sacred.

Life is Inter-connected

Many faith traditions and philosophies have noted that all life is interconnected. The rise of knowledge and information in the modern world raises this concept to incomprehensible levels of complexity. One well known example from chaos theory is the notion of a butterfly flapping its wings in one part of the world ultimately affecting the weather in another part of world. Therefore, science affirms what faith and logic have held- that there is an interconnected web of life on the planet. That web is still far beyond our understanding. A century ago John Muir wrote,

> "When we try to pick out anything by itself we find it hitched
> to everything else in the universe" (Muir Words 63).

One of the weaknesses of Western thought is our compartmentalized approach to so many issues. One of the sad commentaries on our way of thinking is the term to describe someone with broad understanding, experience and education-"Renaissance Man", referring to a time, centuries ago. We live in an age of specialists who often lack the broad understanding to see the interconnections and thereby solve the larger scale problems.

Err on the Side of Life

When it comes to regulation on environmental issues, the common practice is take the strictest position in the effort to eliminate risk. The common phrase is, 'Err on the side of caution.' The problem with this position is that ultimately it is a logical impossibility- you cannot prove a negative. I cannot prove to you the fountain pen sitting on my desk will never hurt someone physically. I think we can all agree that there is very little likelihood it would, but, I cannot prove it. The ethic of a reverence for life would guide us to err on the side of life. Life is full of risks and there are always tradeoffs. We cannot eliminate risk completely. We can chose to use a reverence for life as a guiding principle and when we make choices to err on the side of life.

As noted Aldo Leopold wrote, "An ethic, ecologically, is a limitation on freedom of action in the struggle for existence" (Leopold 238).This is an important point as long as we understand that it comes from outside the natural order, as Schweitzer reminds us. The coyote does not limit his freedom in hunting rabbits. Leopold further defines good as what is good for the land, which is his matrix for life, and bad as what is bad for the land. Schweitzer defines good and evil in a similar way, using 'reverence for life' as his matrix.

Schweitzer's Reverence for Life is a key principle in addressing the environmental problems that have developed since his time. It is non-sectarian and cross-cultural. Reverence for life will still leave us with many difficult choices to make. But, it is the perfect starting point for dialogue. Does something enhance life? Then it is good and should be encouraged. Does something take from life? Then it is bad and should be opposed.

Forward Spin

A journalist friend of mine once mentioned most speakers and writers lack 'forward spin.' "Forward spin?" I asked. "Yes," she said, "the direction on how listeners and readers can respond to the author's work."

What do I hope to accomplish by writing this book? I'd like to--inject some common sense into our dialogue on the environment

-encourage producers that they are not crazy. The system is crazy.

-I'd like to encourage participants in our national and now, international dialogue to find balance on environmental issues.

When I teach Critical Thinking we explore how Either/Or thinking is usually a logical fallacy. Instead of *Either* a healthy environment *Or* a healthy economy how can we find balance for both? It's not about making a buck. If we are going to help people out of poverty and have the resources to care for the environment we are going to need a healthy economy.

If we are going to do this, let's do it right. If we are really going to care for the environment, let's care for the environment.

Let's discuss the reasonable conservation and use of natural resources.

Let's get serious about public education. Let's show people how their personal choices affect the planet—and others.

Let's address materialism. There's more to life than the stuff we have.

Let's bag the Precautionary Principle and agree to a reasonable way to assess risk.

Let's stop being driven by fear.

There is a lot of work to be done. Will you join me?

-locally: there is garbage to pick up and river ways to clean. My friend Sam, in Mendota, is always looking for help.

-regionally: there are watershed and air quality issues to address.

-nationally and globally: we must talk about how to define reasonable use of our natural resources.

There are thousands of issues to address and conversations that must take place. I don't pretend to solve all these problems in a few pages. But, the principles in this book can help in solving the problems we face.

Will you join me?

Acknowledgements

As much as I like rugged individualism and the image of the Lone Ranger, I could not have written this book by myself. For starters, I am the worst proofreader of my own work. I deeply appreciate my wife, Sheryl, my son-in-law, Will Arvance and our neighbor Donna Burdine for their patient attention to detail and wise editorial suggestions. Thank you all.

Alfreda Sebasto is responsible for the spark of inspiration for this book and the original essay from which it came. My neighbors and my employees tend to roll their eyes when environmental issues, or environmental rules and regs come up. During one of our irregular visits for coffee Alfreda encouraged me to do more than talk about it. She encouraged me to put pen to paper. When I hit a rough spot while writing she would spur me on. Thanks Alfreda.

References

Austin, Richard Cartwright, Beauty of the Lord; Awakening the Senses, Atlanta: John Knox Press, 1988.

Avery, Dennis, Saving the Planet with Pesticides and Plastics, Indianapolis Indiana: Hudson Institute, 1995.

Badke, William B., Project Earth, Portland, Oregon: Multnomah Press, 1991.

Berry, Wendell, What Are People For?, New York: North Point Press, 1990.

Blas, Javier, Father of Green Revolution Saved Millions of Loves, http://www.ft.com/cms/s/0/83eb2534-a075-11de-b9ef-00144feabdc0.html#axzz2AbsOPo9I

Brand, Stewart, Whole Earth Discipline: An Ecopragmatist Manifesto, New York: Viking, 2009.

Brinkley, Douglas, The Wilderness Warrior: Theodore Roosevelt and the Crusade for America, New York: Harper Books, 2009.

Brody, Jane, "Scientist at Work: Bruce N. Ames; Strong Views on Origins of Cancer", New York Times, 05 July 1994. <http://www.nytimes.com/1994/07/05/science/scientist-at-work-bruce-n-ames-strong-views-on-origins-of-cancer.html?pagewanted=all&src=pm>

California Water Institute, http://www.californiawater.org/docs/CIT_AWU_Report_v2.pdf

Campolo, Tony, How to Rescue the Earth, Without Worshipping Nature, Nashville: Thomas Nelson, 1992.

Costa, Rebecca, The Watchman's Rattle: Thinking Our Way Out of Extinction, New York, Van Guard Press, 2010.

Covey, Stephen, Principle-Centered Leadership: Audio Learning System, Provo, Utah: Covey Leadership Center, 1992.

Cravens, Gwyneth, Power to Save the World: The Truth About Nuclear Energy, New York: Alfred A. Knopf, 2007.

Crichton, Michael, State of Fear, New York: Harper Collins, 2004.

de Bell, Garrett, The Environmental Handbook, New York: Ballantine, 1970.

Dobson, Andrew, The Green Reader: Essays Toward a Sustainable Society, San Francisco, Mercury House, 1991.

Eldridge, John, Wild at Heart, Nashville: Nelson Books, 2001.

Eldridge, John and Stasi, Captivating, Nashville: Nelson Books, 2005.

Fahrni, Dieter, An Outline History of Switzerland: From the Origins to the Present Day, Zurich, Pro Helvetia, 1997.

Fisher, Roger Ury, William, Getting to Yes! "Seek Options for Mutual Gain," New York: Penguin Books, 1991.

Gandhi, Mohandas K., Gandhi: An Autobiography, Boston: Beacon Press, 1957.

Garcia, Deborah Koons, Symphony of the Soil, selected clips, Lily Films, 2010.

Gore, Albert, Earth in the Balance, Boston: Houghton Mifflin, 1992.

Glieck, James, Chaos: Making a New Science, New York, Penguin Books, 1988.

Holbreich, Mark, et.al, Amish children living in northern Indiana have a very low prevalence of allergic sensitization, Journal of Allergy and Clinical Immunology, 19 April 2012. http://www.jacionline.org/article/S0091-6749(12)00519-2/fulltext

Kaufman, Wallace, No Turning Back: Dismantling the Fantasies of Environmental Thinking, New York: Basic Books, 1994.

Hernandez, Daniela, Access Doesn't Lead to Healthy Eating, LA Times, 17 July 2011. http://articles.latimes.com/2011/jul/17/health/la-he-food-deserts-20110712

Howard, Phillip K., The Death of Common Sense: How Law is Suffocating America, New York: Warner Books, 1994.

Howitt, Richard, et al., Measuring the Employment Impact of Water Reductions, http://ewccalifornia.org/reports/MeasuringEmploymentImpacts-092909.pdf

James, Jennifer, Thinking in the Future Tense, New York, Touchstone Books, 1996.

Joy, Charles R., Albert Schweitzer: An Anthology, Boston: Beacon Press, 1947.

Kalam, Apj Abdul, India 202: A Vision for the New Millenium, New York, Viking, 1998.

Kierkegaard, Soren, Fear and Trembling/ Repetition, Princeton: Princeton University Press, 1983.

Lancet. 2001 Oct 6;358(9288):1129-33.

Leopold, Aldo, The Sand County Almanac, New York: Ballantine Books, 1970.

Meyer, Art and Jocelle, Earthkeepers: Environmental Perspectives on Hunger, Poverty, And Injustice, Scottsdale Pennsylvania: Herald Press, 1991.

Moore, Patrick, Environmentalism for the 21st Century, http://www.green-spirit.com/21st_century.cfm

Muir, John, The Mountains of California, Golden, Colorado: Fulcrum Press, 1988.

, John Muir: In His Own Words, Lafayette, CA, Great West Books, 1988.

NPR, Fear Dominates Discussion on Nuclear Power, 22 March 2011, http://www.npr.org/2011/03/22/134755650/Fear-Stokes-Discussions-On-Nuclear-Power

NPR, Saving the Spotted Owl: Benefits of Recovery Effort Remain Complex, Controversial, 5 August 2004, http://www.npr.org/templates/story/story.php?storyId=3815722

Olasky, Marvin, The Tragedy of American Compassion, Washington, DC: Regenery, 1992.

Postrel, Virginia, Of Mice and Men: Bruce Ames Interview, Reason Magazine, http://reason.com/archives/1994/11/01/of-mice-and-men, 1994.

Powell, John Wesley, Seeing Things Whole, Washington, DC: Island Press, 2001.

Ray, Dixie Lee, Environmental Overkill: Whatever Happened to Common Sense?, Washington DC: Regnery Press, 1993.

Reisner, Marc, Cadillac Desert, New York: Penguin Books, 1986.

Rollins, Ed, Bare Knuckles and Back Rooms: My Life in American Politics, New York: Broadway Books, 1996.

Roosevelt, Theodore, Theodore Roosevelt: An Autobiography, New York: Da Capo Press, 1985.

Sanera, Michael and Shaw, Jane S., Facts not Fear: A Parent's Guide to Teaching Children About the Environment, Washington DC" Regenery, 1996.

Schlesinger, Arthur, Jr., The Age of Jackson, Boston: Little Brown and Co. 1945.

Schlaes, Amity, The Forgotten Man, New York: Harper Perennial, 2007.

Schweitzer, Albert, Out of My Life and Thought, New York: Holt, 1937.

, Reverence for Life, New York: Harper and Row 1969.

, The Philosophy of Civilization, New York: MacMillan, 1959.

Sen, Amartya, The Amartya Sen and Jean Dreze Omnibus, New Delhi: Oxford University Press, 1999.

Shultz, Howard, Onward, New York: Rodale, 2011

Smith, Adam, An Inquiry Into the Nature and Causes of the Wealth of Nations, Amazon: Kindle Edition.

Stossel, John, Are We Scaring Ourselves to Death?, ABC News, 1994.

Szalavitz, Maia, Ten Ways We Get the Odds Wrong, http://www.psychologytoday.com/articles/200712/10-ways-we-get-the-odds-wrong

Thoreau, Henry David, Walden and Other Writings, New York: Bantam Books, 1970.

Van Matre, Steve and Weiler, The Bill, Earth Speaks: An Acclimatization Journal, Warrenville, Illinois: Institute of Earth Education, 1983.

White, Lynn Townsend, Jr, "The Historical Roots of Our Ecologic Crisis", Science, Vol. 155 (Number 3767), March 10, 1967, pp. 1203–1207.

Whitman, Walt, Leaves of Grass, New York, Barnes and Noble, 1993.

Wilson, E. O., The Future of Life, New York: Vintage, 2002.

Zhao, Yong, Catching Up or Leading the Way, Alexandria, Virginia: ASCD, 2009.

Appendix

Ten Reasons I Question Environmentalists
By Paul H. Betancourt
Fresno Business Journal October, 2005

I mentioned to a friend that I'll start believing environmentalists on issues here in the Valley when they stop taking water out of Hetch Hetchy in Yosemite National Park for drinking water in San Francisco. To me it is an issue of integrity. You can't abuse the environment to your benefit and then tell me how I should interact with the environment. She suggested I do a David Letterman style Top Ten list. So here we go-

For the record, I need to note that I think most of the environmentalists I have met are sincere. I call them true believers, not to mock them but because I do find that their passion is very similar to new converts to faith. Many are just as dogmatic. They are the New Puritans.

Ten Reasons I Question Environmentalists

#10-I'll start believing San Francisco environmentalists when they stop taking their drinking water from a national park.

#9- I'll start believing the French on energy and environmental issues when they turn off their nuclear reactors. Either nuclear power is bad, or it is good. Nuclear power cannot be good in France and bad in the US.

#8-I'll start believing Europeans about organic farming when they stop chain smoking.

[I am constantly amazed how my European friends are so concerned about possible carcinogens in their food and yet they are such heavy smokers.]

#7-I'll start believing environmentalists when they start offering solutions. What I usually see is a presentation of a problem and then they jump up and down and tell us to stop it. For example, they will tell us how bad over population is. Then tell us to stop it. What kind of solution is that? It would be nice if the solutions made sense. One suggestion they had about dust on dirt roads was to water the dirt roads every day. Do you know how many miles of dirt roads there are in Fresno County? Do you know how much water that would take? Do you know how many of those roads have no traffic at all during the day? That wasn't much of solution. Watering the roads we use makes a lot more sense. But, the farmers had to suggest that, the enviros didn't figure that one out.

#6-Crisis du Jour: When was the last time you heard about the ozone layer or the rainforest? Remember when that was all we heard about? Did the problem go away? Did it get solved? I'll start believing the environmentalists when they stick with an issue until it is solved not skip from one issue to the next depending on their Hollywood celebrity or rock concert.

#5- I'll start believing environmentalists when they start doing effective public education. After nearly 40 years they have failed to develop effective environmental awareness. People say they are environmentalists then they drive big SUV's. There is a disconnect.

Public education is slow and tedious work. But, as Emile Durkhiem said a century ago-"When people are moral no laws are necessary. When people are not moral no law are sufficient." The point is that when we have a well developed public awareness about the environment we would need endless laws and endless debates to scare us into compliance.

#4-I'll start believing the environmentalists when they stop acting like Chicken Little. I am now hearing reports that global temperatures will go up 20 degrees and the ocean levels will rise a meter in this century. Perhaps. But, they have been so wrong for so long I wonder how they have any credibility left. Malthus, two hundred years ago, and Paul Ehrlich, thirty years ago, said that population growth would outstrip our ability to feed ourselves. They were wrong. How can we believe these alarming claims when they have been so wrong for so long?

#3-I'll believe the Environmentalists when they have a view of the Big Picture. They teach us that life is an inter-connected web and then they focus on their special interest. I have sat in too many meetings where specialists have dug in their heels, not willing to compromise or even discuss any other issues until their concern was fully settled. Environmental problems are, by nature, system wide problems. They need big picture solutions. For example, hybrid cars will save gas. What are we planning to do with all those used hybrid batteries?

#2-I will start believing the environmentalists when they start living themselves the life style they recommend for the rest of us. I really respect the advocates who actually ride their bicycles. Don't live a modern lifestyle and then complain about everyone else living one.

And finally,

#1- I'll believe the environmentalists when they realize they have already won.

The air is cleaner and our rivers don't catch fire like they once did. There is tremendous public support for the environment. The tide is in their favor. They should celebrate their victory and lead us onward and upward instead of beating us over the head and dragging us from one crisis to the next.

I want to be a caretaker of the environment. When I used to hike as a kid I was taught to leave my campsite cleaner than when I got there. I am looking for practical solutions to the problems we face. I'll start believing my environmental friends when they start being reasonable.

How This Farmer Learned to Love Pesticides
By Paul H. Betancourt
Fresno Bee September 17, 1996.

No one would want to farm without chemicals more than I do. When I came to the Valley from San Diego in 1981 I had dreams of small-scale organic farming and all the city dwellers prejudice against pesticides, herbicides and fungicides.While I may not like them anymore than before, I have learned that used properly, farm chemicals can be safe, effective and indeed one of the foundations of our modern society. The fear industrial complex of professional worriers has done a good job convincing the public that their food is poisoned and all farm chemicals cause cancer. No one stops to think, if our food is poisoned, then why are we living longer, healthier lives than our ancestors?

The question each one of us needs to ask ourselves is, are we better off or worse off by the use of the pesticides and the other tools of modern agriculture?

Dr. Bruce Ames, a biochemist in Berkeley, says, "I think pesticides lower the cancer rate.Ames bases his position on the fact that a balanced diet with plenty of fruits and vegetables will do more to prevent cancer than any risks from the chemicals used to produce that food.

Ames also notes that our food is full of naturally occurring carcinogens. A peanut butter sandwich is 100 times more carcinogenic than a fish full of DDT. A glass of cola, coffee or wine is 1,000 times more carcinogenic than water from the wells in Silicon Valley that were shut down due to groundwater contamination. This doesn't mean we should ignore the health concerns from using pesticides. But, we must put our fears in perspective. One of the assumptions we have is that we can have all the benefits of modern agriculture without the risk. As Dr. Ames says, "the price you pay for living in a modern, industrial society is a few parts per billion of something in the water. Just eat a good diet and don't worry. After all, worrying probably causes cancer too.

Real concerns about the use of pesticides are clouded by the nonsense of the fear mongers. It is appropriate that we assess farm chemicals for their safety to ensure public health. But we must not be prejudiced against nor afraid of pesticide use.

The industry must continually show the public, its customers, that these chemicals can be used safely and that we take their safety seriously. The public must acknowledge farm chemicals are one of the basic tools of modern society.

As Dixie Lee Ray, former Washington governor, says,

"Sometime in the future, when the accomplishments of the 20th century are recorded for posterity, it may finally be acknowledged that our greatest achievement by far has been the introduction of high-tech, high-yield agriculture."

High-tech, high-yield agriculture is at the foundation of modern society. Those who believe that we can have all the benefits of modern agriculture without any of the modern tools are wrong.

Ten Reasons-Listening to Nobel Winners
By Paul H. Betancourt
Copyright, 2011

While balance is important, it can also be static. If there is anything that is true about modern life it is that it is moving forward. The question is, how do we move forward while protecting our environment? How do we embrace technologies like modern medicine and all the good they do and protect the environment? How do we lift people out of poverty, increase our standards of living and protect the environment?

Can you see what I meant in Reason One? The enviros have already won. Everything we want to achieve as a race will take the environment into account. So, how do we balance care for the environment and progress?

It is easy for me to say our guiding principles should be, "a healthy environment and a healthy economy." But, what does that look like in practice? I think part of the answer can be found in the work of Elinor Ostrum, 2009 co-winner of the Nobel Prize in Economics. A lot of the challenges in current environmental policy center on natural resource issues. I address some of these issues in Reason 10. Ostrum's work focuses on Common Pool Resources (CPR's), and the government institutions to manage these resources.

Ostrum's work is not limited to the Western world or merely to our time. In her 1990 book Governing the Commons she also studies institutions that manage Common Pool Resources in Sri Lanka, the Philippines, Turkey and Japan. She also studies groundwater management in Southern California in the 1960's as well as historic irrigation management in Spain and historic timber management in Switzerland. Ostrum's conclusion is there are significant structures and policies that can be entered in to voluntarily by resource entrepreneurs. These agreements can be monitored internally and/or by governments.

Ostrum's "Design Principles and Institutional Performances" for successful use of Common Pool Resources include-"Clear boundaries and memberships-individuals or households who have rights to withdraw resource units from the CPR must be clearly defined, as must the boundaries of the CPR itself.

Congruent roles-Congruence between appropriation and provision rules and local conditions Appropriation rules restricting time, place, technology and/or quantity of resource units are related to local conditions and to provision rules requiring labor, material and. Or money.

Collective choice arrangements- Most individuals affected by the operational rules can participate in modifying the operational rules.

Monitoring- Monitors who actively audit CPR conditions and appropriator behaviors, are accountable to the appropriators or are the appropriators.

Graduated Sanctions- Appropriators who violate operational rules are likely to be assessed graduated sanctions (depending on the seriousness and context of the offense) by other appropriators, by officials accountable to these appropriators, or by both.

Conflict Resolution Mechanisms- Appropriators and their officials have rapid access to low cost local arenas to resolve conflicts among appropriators or between appropriators and officials.

Regional rights to organize-The rights of appropriators to devise their own isntitutions are not challenged by external government authorities.

Nested assets- Appropriation, provision, monitoring, enforcement, conflict resolution and government activities are organized in multiple layers of nested enterprises. (Ostrum p. 90-102)

Please remember these principles are not academic theory, they are time tested principles. The point of Ostrum's work is that we have a Nobel proven alternative to Hardin's Tragedy of the Commons scenario. Since publication in 1968 the image of the 'Tragedy of the Commons' has driven people to conclude that resource entrepreneurs cannot be trusted to use resources in a responsible and sustainable manner.

It is true there are many examples of clear cutting and over grazing to point at in support of Hardin's thesis. What Ostrum shows us is there are also many examples of resource users, in many different cultures and over long periods of time who managed Common Pool Resources in the desired sustainable manner.

The obvious question is, which model will prevail as we move forward? Hardin's pessimistic model and the call for more centralized control? Or. Ostrum's model, rooted in history that shows a way forward?

As a farmer I find it ironic that people use Hardin's work to call for more centralized control. It is ironic because while there is deep public support for family farmers in many places, the environmental controls demanded by big government solutions drive smaller farmers out of business with their increased paperwork and higher capital costs. It is the large corporations who are tempted to clear cutting or strip mining because that kind of efficiency that drives modern industry. But, it also the large corporations that can afford to have environmental compliance officers, where a family farm rarely has the time to commit to that in the rush of daily life. Ostrum's model can be utilized by family sized operations for farming, fishing, timber and grazing when they work together in community.

Yes, I need to turn a profit to make a living on my farm. But, unlike many industries farmers rarely look at quarterly reports. Our timeline is much longer. I like the definition of sustainability that comes from my fellow farmers in Australia, "We as a family, on our farm, in the future: (Vanclay 215). That doesn't sound like people tempted by the Tragedy of the Commons does it?

As I mentioned earlier, another irony of the lack of balance in centralized, big government solution sis illustrated by Al Gore in his *Earth in the Balance*. Two of Gore's great examples of environmental disaster in strong, centralized governments- the Aral Sea in the former Soviet Union and the air quality in Romania. George Bailey also noted massive environmental degradation in East Germany that came to light as Germany began to reunite after the fall of communism. (Bailey 488).

Under communism entrepreneurs of any type had little opportunity. Common pool resources were managed by the state, obviously with little thought to sustainability. Instead of worrying about a potential Tragedy of the Commons in the West under free market capitalism critics would benefit from considering the legacy of resource management under centralized government control. It is not an automatic panacea.

Resources

Bailey, George, Germans: The Biography of Obsessions, New York, Free Press, 1991.

Gore, Al, Earth in the Balance, New York, Houghton Mifflin, 1992.

Ostrum, Elinor, Governing the Commons: The Evolution of Institutions for Collective Action, Cambridge, Cambridge University Press, 1990.

Vanclay, F., Social principles for agricultural extension to assist in the promotion of natural resource management. Australian Journal of Experimental Agriculture, 2004, 44, 213-22.

Index

CPSIA information can be obtained at www.ICGtesting.com
Printed in the USA
BVOW02s0503050913

330271BV00003B/399/P